Jupiter:
The Planet of Fortune

Jupiter: The Planet of Fortune

A Research Work on The Astrological Aspects of Jupiter

Author

Ajay Srivastava

Jyotirvid, Jyotirvisharad

First Edition, 2024

Published by:

Ajay Kumar Srivastava

45, Awas Vikas Colony, Betiya Hata,

Gorakhpur – 273001 (U.P.), India

Mobile No.: +91-9867837184

Disclaimer: This publication contains the opinions and ideas of its author and is designed to provide useful information in regard to the subject matter covered. The author and the publisher specifically disclaim any responsibility for liability, loss, or risk, personal or otherwise, that is incurred as a consequence, directly or indirectly, of the use and application of any of the contents of this book.

<u>Lord Jupiter</u>

<u>Prayer</u>

देवानां च ऋषीणां च गुरुं काञ्चनसंनिभम् ।

बुद्धिभूतं त्रिलोकेशं तं नमामि बृहस्पतिम् ।।

|| Devaanaanca rishinaanca gurum kaancana sannibham
Buddhi bhutam trilokesham tam namaami Brihaaspatim
Om Gurave Namah ||

(**Translation**: I bow down to Jupiter, teacher of gods and sages, the greatest treasure, and the most intelligent of all creation. Om, I bow down to Jupiter.)

Dedication

I dedicate this book to my father (Late) Sri R.A.L Srivastava who taught me to be an independent, courageous and determined person, and my mother Maya Srivastava whose unconditional love and support always help me to overcome all the obstacles in my life. She has a selfless spirit and served others throughout her life. Her immense patience is peerless and she always inspires me to go ahead.

Preface

Human life on earth is meant for expansion, without expansion life has no meaning. Swami Vivekananda has said that, "Expansion is life, contraction is death". Nature expands everything, the force of life is visible everywhere. Every time a new life is taking birth and nature keeps on maintaining and developing. This energy of life goes on continuously.

The fetus growing in the mother's womb gradually becomes a child and the child becomes young, then the young become old. Everything is in continuity and everything is expanding. It is a journey that everyone is on. So, the question arises in the mind what the force behind such expansion.

When I started learning astrology, I found that planets play an important role in every aspect of human life. This subtle energy affects everything on earth and we are connected with these forces. Hindu astrology considers the influence of only nine planets and among them Jupiter is the most important and auspicious planet. Life means expansion and every expansion on earth is controlled by Jupiter. Without his blessings no one can take even a step in any expansionary activity. A strong Jupiter is necessary for growth and to fulfil all the auspicious purpose of life. Jupiter is an asset which every person must accumulate but people are interested in accumulating worthless material things.

They forget that the planet of benevolence also provide protection shield which help us to move our legs on the unknown path. But when the protective shield is removed, then the person is unable to cope with unknown dangers.

I learned that this planetary order in the solar system has an important meaning and everything here plays a vital role in the proper functioning of the universal activities. I also learned that astronomy is also important for learning astrology. I realized that it is difficult to understand the properties and functioning of planets without understanding astronomy.

I have spent two decades of my career in financial research and doing research has always been my passion. I am never satisfied with a superficial observation and always try to go deep into the matter and find the root cause. The passion to do financial research is shifted to do astrological research and about two years before I started writing my books and blogs. I analyzed the horoscopes of various individuals and I came to know that "Jupiter - The most Auspicious Planet", play a very important role in our lives.

I went deeper and found that somewhere my opinion is not matching with the prevailing opinion. I found that the knowledge of our ancient texts is written in sutras (codes) and different people interpret them differently according to their experiences.

My findings and experiences are far different, so I decided to collect all my data and decided to write a book on Jupiter.

I pray and bow to Lord Jupiter and believe that this book cannot be completed without his blessings, who provide proper direction all times.

It is astrology that changed my life forever and a person who did not believe in astrology at all till a few years ago, has been able to complete this book today.

I give special thanks to my younger brother Abhay Srivastava for their valuable suggestions, without which such work would not have been possible.

I thank God for completing this book. It is not possible for me to convert my thoughts into words without the grace of "The Almighty".

Ajay Srivastava

10th Feb 2023

Navi Mumbai

Acknowledgement

The existence of this book would not have been possible without the help of my wife Seema and my daughter Saanvi. They provided me enough help to write down my thoughts which I have collected so far in my life. My wife has been instrumental as an illustrator and proof-reader and has given me enough insights to write the matter in a simple and explanatory manner.

Ajay Srivastava

Contents

Chapter 1

Introduction

Jupiter is considered to be the most benefic planet in astrology. Jupiter is known as the prime minister in the planetary cabinet. In Sanskrit, Jupiter is known as "Brihaspati" and a master to the gods. Jupiter is a karaka of luck, wealth, and wisdom. Jupiter represents mantra, sacred scriptures, religion, and philosophy. Jupiter bestows the person with children and represents the expansion of the family. It rules over finance and represents administration and economic activity. It is called "The Planet of Fortune".

Namesake: The planet is named "Jupiter" after the king of gods in Roman mythology.

Exaltation and Debilitation: Jupiter is exalted at 5° in Cancer and debilitated at 5° in Capricorn.

Lord of Two Signs: Jupiter is the lord of two signs Sagittarius and Pisces, where the former is its positive sign represents the masculine aspect, and the latter is its negative sign represents the feminine aspect.

Mooltrikona Sign: First 10 degrees of Sagittarius is Jupiter's Mooltrikona sign.

Direction and Digbala: The direction of Jupiter is North-East; It gets directional strength (Digbala) in the 1st house and weakness in the 7th house.

Day: Jupiter is the lord of Thursday, as per Hora. However, in planetary order, it is the fifth closest planet to the Sun and comes after Mars.

Vedic Mantra: Om Bum Brihaspataye Namaha

Beej Mantra: Om Graang Greeng Graung Sah Gurave Namah

The Birth of Jupiter: According to Navagraha Purana, sage Angiras wants an exceptionally talented and wise son. Therefore, as advised by the sage Narada, he along with his wife Shraddha prayed Agnideva with full devotion and performed Agnikarya - a best-liked homa for Lord Agni. With the blessings of Lord Agni, soon Shraddha got pregnant and gave birth to a brilliant boy.

On the day of the naming ceremony Sage Angiras uttered the name of his son "Brihaspati". Tridev (Bharma, Vishnu, and Mahesh) blessed the boy, and on behalf of that Sage Narada announced that due to his intense wisdom, Brihaspati will get a very special position in the planetary cabinet, would be known as Devguru and have a very special place among the nine planets.

After completing his education Lord Brihaspati became the advisor of the gods and started imparting knowledge to the seekers.

Gemstone: Jupiter gemstone is yellow sapphire and the metal is gold.

Maturity Age: Jupiter's maturity age is 16 years; It means after attaining such age the planet starts providing its results.

Classification: Jupiter is considered a sattvic planet. It is a masculine and brahmin caste planet. Its colour is yellow, the stone is yellow sapphire or topaz and the metal is gold. It represents a gentle tendency and sweet taste. It represents fat constituents and tall height. It deals with medium clothes and living beings. It indicates Hemant season (20th Nov. to 19th Jan. approx.) and evenly momentum.

Nature: Jupiter is a watery planet. It is a highly benefic planet and represents optimism, buoyancy, and expansion. The planet of abundance is noble and benevolent. It provides dignity, fame, and reputation. It indicates honesty, faith, morality, spirituality, and devotion.

Element: Jupiter rules over ether element (Aakash Tattva).

Symbol: The symbol of Jupiter is "♃".

The Number "2": In India people like to start anything with '2' and then as a multiple of '2'. The symbol of '2' invokes the energy

Chapter 2

Astronomy

The study of astronomy is important for understanding astrology. Astronomy studies the celestial bodies, while astrology studies the effect of planetary energy on human life and on Earth. This energy is not visible to us, so many people completely reject astrology, of which I was one too until a few years ago. It is a matter of experience, if one does not experience such subtle energy then astrology cannot be known through logic.

The universe is full of energy and the transits of celestial bodies always change this energy level. This human body is a part of existence and nothing here exists in isolation. Each planet has an important meaning and its impact on human life we cannot understand, without understanding astronomy.

Following is a brief astronomical description of the planet Jupiter.

The Planet: Jupiter is the largest planet in the solar system and the fifth planet closest to the Sun. It is more than twice as massive as all the other planets combined. Jupiter's immense volume could hold more than 1,300 Earths. After the Moon and Venus, Jupiter is the third brightest object which can be visible in the night sky.

Jupiter has a very powerful gravity that attracts many of the comets and asteroids to hit it, rather than other planets.

Distance from Sun: 778.3 million km (5.203 astronomical units, or AU)

Moon: Jupiter has 79 known moons. The four important moons of Jupiter known as Galilean moons; lo, Europa, Ganymede, and Callisto. Europa may have water on it and is currently being studied.

Size: The diameter of the planet is 142,800 km and the radius is 69,900 km. Its diameter is more than 11 times compared of Earth.

Period of Rotation: Jupiter rotates once on its axis every 10 earth hours. It means one day on Jupiter takes only about 10 earth hours.

Period of Revolution: Jupiter makes one complete orbit around the Sun in about 12 years (4,333 Earth days) and stays in a sign for about a year.

Opposition: When in opposition, a planet is on the opposite side of Earth from the Sun, i.e., all are in an alignment. Jupiter comes into opposition approximately every 13 months and it is in a new zodiac sign every year. So, Jupiter's opposition comes about a month later each year.

Axis: Its axis is tilted by 3.13°. So, seasonal fluctuations are very minimal.

Temperature: Jupiter's average temperature is -234° F (-145° C).

Rings: Like Saturn, Jupiter also has rings, and they are divided into three parts, but they are notably faint.

Surface and Structure: Jupiter is known as a gas giant planet and doesn't have a solid surface, but it has a solid core about the size of Earth at its center. It is made mostly out of hydrogen (90%) and helium (10%). The planet often changes its color due to clouds of gases.

Due to its strong gravitational force, a person would weigh 2.5 times more than Earth on Jupiter. Due to its fast-spinning Jupiter's magnetic field is 16 to 54 times as powerful as that of the Earth.

The Great Red Spot: Jupiter is a turbulent and windy planet. The Great Red Spot is one of its most prominent features of this planet and has been around for at least 350 years. It is big enough to hold two Earths.

Chapter 3

Jupiter in Astrology

Every planet has important meaning in astrology and understanding of such knowledge provides us valuable insights. Jupiter being the largest planet in the solar system represents expansion and children are the expansion of our life, children are our future, Jupiter is the karaka of children and represents the future. When we analyze the position of Jupiter in both Lagna Kundali and Navamsha Kundali it provides a clear vision as to which direction the fate of a person is pulling him, as Navamsha is also called Bhagya and as we move ahead in life our destiny draws us. Therefore, understanding the various aspects of Jupiter is very important and it helps us to move on the unknown path of life.

Devguru Brihaspati bestows education, knowledge, intelligence and wealth to a person. Knowingly or unknowingly, when we start any auspicious work in life, we remember Lord Jupiter. In India, when we go to do any auspicious work, we apply turmeric tilak on our forehead and seek the blessings of Lord Brihaspati. People deposit money in their lockers, actually they are accumulating Jupiter, but Jupiter represents sky, hence wealth can't be locked at one place. People tend to collect the things of Jupiter because they want auspicious things in their surroundings. Jupiter represents many things in life, some important ones are the following;

Physical Appearance: A person influenced by Jupiter has good physical growth in puberty and no one cannot ignore such growth. The body of a person influenced by Jupiter is thick and heavy.

Colour: Yellow

Body Parts: Jupiter represents liver, pituitary gland, circulation of blood in the arteries, pancreas, hips, thighs, and body fat.

Diseases: Problem in liver, flatulence, jaundice, diabetes, eczema, hernia, dropsy, dyspepsia, etc.

Animals: Jupiter represents animals like horse, ox, elephant, sheep, unicorn, stag and domestic animals.

Birds: It represents eagle, peacock, pheasant, dove etc.

Natural Karaka: Jupiter is the karaka of 2nd, 5th, 9th, 10th and 11th house.

Metals and Gems: Jupiter represents gold, platinum, yellow sapphire and topaz.

Places: Jupiter represents temples and religious places, schools and colleges, educational institutions, universities, legislative assembly, law-court, big pompous buildings, bank buildings, charitable institutions, hospitals, asylums. It represents places where money, jewels and important items are deposited, like; treasury room, locker room, store room etc.

Products: Jupiter represents all fatty and sweet products like ghee, butter, cream, all sweet flavored products, honey, dates, squash, pulses, pumpkin, beet, apricots, figs, banana, etc.

Tree: Peepal tree, Banana tree, Devdaar tree

Wealth: Jupiter is karaka for wealth. A strong Jupiter bestows the person with wealth. There are four elements – Fire, Earth, Air and Water. Abundant of wealth is available in water and earth but fire and air have no wealth. Therefore, placement of Jupiter in watery or earthy sign is necessary for creation of abundant wealth.

The 2nd house is the house of savings and family, if Jupiter is placed is any watery or earthy signs (other than capricorn) in this house then person will be a wealthy person and able to save money. If the same Jupiter is placed in any fiery or airy sign then the person will earn money but savings are difficult, and such a person may have a large family. Any connection between 2nd and 11th house is good because 11th is the house of income.

If Jupiter is placed in 12th house which is the house of expenditure and in an airy sign, such person will spend unnecessarily and always looking for money, no matter how much wealth he possesses.

It is necessary to analyze the placement of Jupiter in house and in which element it is placed both in the Natal chart and Navamsha chart. Also, the position of Jupiter from the Sun and the Moon is necessary to check because the conclusion cannot be taken by analyzing only one aspect.

Aspects: Jupiter means direction and support. Devguru Brihaspati always provides necessary direction to the person to go ahead always in the right path.

Jupiter's aspect is indeed highly beneficial. Jupiter has three aspects 5th, 7th, and 9th. In the natural zodiac, 1st-5th-9th signs are the same element as Fire-Fire-Fire, and so on, it indicates a natural flow of energy. Hence, the 5th and 9th aspects are highly beneficial. In the natural zodiac 1st and 7th elements support each other. Like Fire is supported by Air (1-7), Earth and Water support each other (2-8). So, Jupiter's 7th aspect is highly supportive.

In which house Jupiter is placed in the natal chart, the 7th to that house and its lord provide necessary support to the person. At the time when every hope is over and there is no sign of rays, then Jupiter provides necessary support to the person.

For example, if Jupiter is placed in Lagna then the person's wife and placement of 7th lord will help the person. If Jupiter is placed in 5th house, then planets in 11th house and placement of 11th lord will help the person. If Jupiter is placed in 12th house, then 6th house and its lord will help the person at the time of crisis in life.

Example Chart 1:

Natal Chart

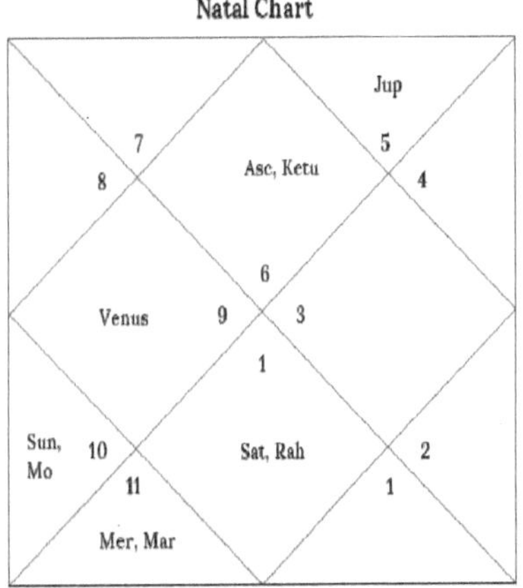

Navamsha Chart

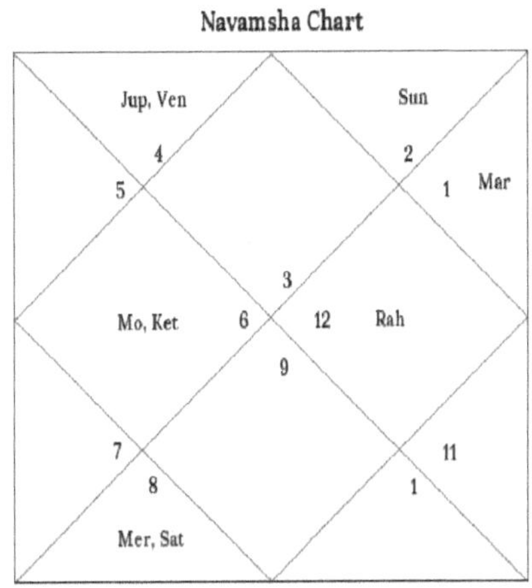

This is the chart of a male born in the year January 1968. In natal chart Jupiter is placed in 12th house in a fiery sign aspecting 6th house and in Navamsha chart it is placed in 2nd house in exaltation. The person told me that once in life he was utterly in need of money and there is no visible source of income and he is in a state of deep frustration then suddenly circumstances changes in his life. A person from his work place offered a good opportunity to him. Analyze his 6th house, Mars represent land, Mercury represent a young person and 6th lord Saturn is placed in 7th house which is the house of partner. A combination all three happened and the person was able to overcome his problem.

Example Chart 2:

Natal Chart

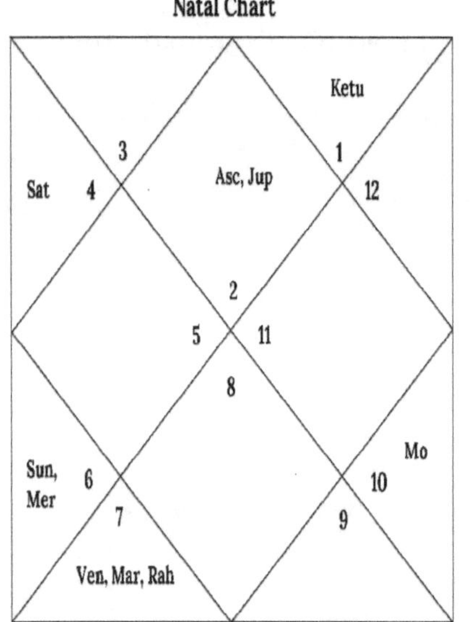

Navamsha Chart

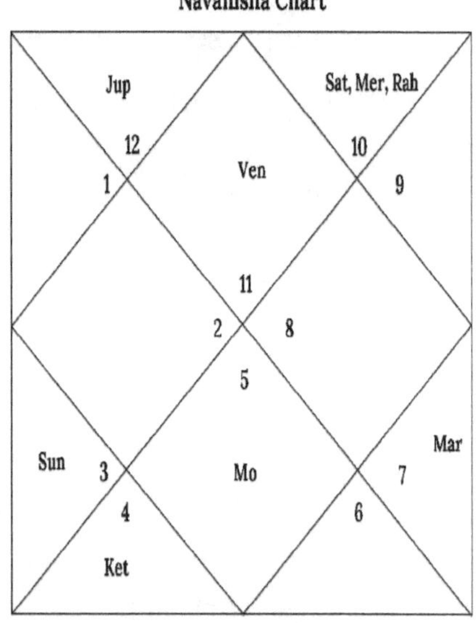

This is the chart of a male born in the year October 1976. In the natal chart, Jupiter is in the ascendant in the Taurus sign and in the Navamsha chart it is placed in the 2nd house in Pisces. A few years before, he had faced a very tough time in his career, and at that time his wife helped him. Examine the 7th house from Jupiter which is again the 7th house, which is the house of spouse and the 7th lord is placed in the 6th house with Venus and Rahu. Venus represents fancy items; Rahu is export, artificial things, and Mars is sales. Circumstances change the life of the person, a combination of all these helped the person and he could overcome such problems in life.

I have seen that help comes in times of trouble, when a person follows the path of righteousness in his life. If the person provides wrong direction to others willingly or for the sack of his enjoyment, if he disrespects his guru, if does not respect knowledge and wisdom of others and feels jealous, if he theft other person's money or cheated others for money, then Jupiter will not provide any support to such a person, even if the person's birth chart is indicating very strong support.

Chapter 4

Puranic Story Related to Jupiter

Many stories related to Jupiter have been written in our texts. Among them, when I read the story of the birth of Mercury, I realized that it is of great importance from the present perspective. In today's highly hectic work culture where everyone is running and people do not have time for others, this story tells a lot and indicates the consequences of such types of culture and environment.

4.1 The Birth of Mercury

The Moon (Chandra Dev) is considered the most beautiful of all the gods in heaven (Devlok). Devraj Indra asked him to gain knowledge from Devguru Brihaspati and become wise. As per the advice of Devraj Indra, he starts going to Brihaspati's palace to gain knowledge where he meets Jupiter's beautiful wife Tara.

Devguru Brihaspati was very busy with the affairs of the kingdom and was unable to give proper time for teaching and also for his wife. In the absence of Jupiter, Tara feels an attraction to the Moon and a relationship develops between them. But Brihaspati could not recognize what mistake he was making. His excessive involvement in the activity of the kingdom and his absence provides both a chance.

Soon, Tara falls in love with Moon and elopes with him. This made Brihaspati very angry and he asked Moon to return his wife but Moon refused. Brihaspati then told Indra that if his wife did not return, he would stop performing all the rituals and providing all the necessary direction for the kingdom. The story goes further that Venus helped the Moon and the possibility of a war between gods and demons intensified. Lord Brahma then intervened in the matter and asked Moon to return Tara.

After such intervention, Moon returned Tara, but Brihaspati refused to accept her, as she was pregnant and Brihaspati said that this child is not mine. Now Tara is helpless, where will she go now, she cannot go back with Moon and her husband is not accepting her. Then, Lord Sun then came to Tara's rescue and said that she could give birth to the child in their palace. Then Mercury was born which is always close to the Sun.

4.2 Significance of The Story

This story has great importance in today's world. This indicates that even a very knowledgeable person can make mistakes if he forgets the principle of balance in life. It is very important to understand the mistakes made by Jupiter;

- Incorrect assessment of priorities

- Excessive involvement in a single activity

- Not giving time to other responsibilities

- Unable to catch the hidden development

- Misjudgment of the current situation due to preconceived notions

Jupiter was unable to understand the attraction of Moon and the consequences of continuing his ignorance towards Tara. He wakes up only when his wife runs away. This story indicates that even a very intelligent person can lose the most favorable thing in his life by being overly involved in some activity and neglecting others.

Everything is balanced in nature. When a person's life becomes imbalanced due to his excessive indulgence, it has to be balanced. So, Jupiter is not the end of the solar system. Then, comes the tough master, "Saturn - The Planet of Balance", which shows the real world to the person and cuts off all the redundancies done by Jupiter.

Chapter 5

Important Characteristics of Jupiter

Devguru Brihaspati always bestows good fortune on a person, by his blessings ignorance and darkness are dispelled and knowledge of light is attained. With that knowledge, a person always takes wise decisions and does not wander in vain. With his blessings, a person becomes wise and is considered a very respected person in the society. The planet of benevolence (Jupiter) bestows a person with many positive traits and qualities, one walks on the path of truth and spirituality and attains divine knowledge.

5.1 Jupiter is Wisdom

Devguru Brihaspati is the lord of wisdom. Without his blessings no one can become a knowledgeable and wise person. We are always looking for wisdom because we want to remove the darkness from our life. Hence, one should never do any act to displease Jupiter.

A strong an unafflicted Jupiter in a chart indicates that the person has done various good deeds in his past lives and is now eligible to take a step towards supreme knowledge.

5.2 Jupiter is Expansion

The biggest planet that rules all the expansionary activities controls all our strategies and big plans. Jupiter's placement in a chart indicates a person will adopt ethical principles and take interest in the expansion of activities related to the house concerned. However, some ancient text says that Jupiter gives bad results for a house in which it is placed and gives good results where its aspects. After reading this I thought why the most benefic planet does not produce good results where it is placed. Later, I realized that there is some hidden meaning in this.

Everything within the limit is good but when it crosses its limit it will create trouble. The planet of expansion also functions in the same manner. Jupiter gives expansion where it is placed, but if the expansion is unnecessary and uncontrolled then it becomes a source of trouble. For example, it is good to eat sugar to the limit, but overeating leads to diabetes. The 6th house indicates taking a loan, the 8th house indicates possession and utilization of money because it is 2nd to the 7th house, and the 12th house indicates its repayment as repaying a loan is an expense for the native. Jupiter in the 6th or the 8th house indicates that the person gets loans easily but if he will take loans beyond his capacity then the repayment of it will create trouble. Jupiter in the 12th house indicates that such a person is unable to control his expenditure and due to his spendthrift nature, he always finds himself in scarcity of money. Mismanagement of debt and expenses means weak Jupiter.

Where Jupiter is placed it provides expansion but too much is bad, and due to this reason, our texts say that where Jupiter is placed it does not produce good results. In fact, every expansion is wrong except the expansion towards God. Therefore, Saturn keeps cutting the expansion done by Jupiter.

5.3 Jupiter is Life

Jupiter represents growth, and the freshwater of Cancer represents life as well as growth. Therefore, Jupiter feels most comfortable in the sign of Cancer and gets exalted here at 5 degrees. Cancer is the fourth sign of the zodiac which is ruled by the Moon. The fourth house also represents the mother's womb. A pregnant woman is the best example of an exalted Jupiter in Cancer. The unborn baby (fetus) growing in the womb floats in the fluid, indicating life expands in the water. Therefore, nothing should ever be done to harm a pregnant woman, otherwise Jupiter of such a person will be destroyed forever and he has to live the life of an unfortunate person for a long time.

In ancient India, a guru's hermitage was always on the bank of a river. The students used to receive knowledge from their guru under the tree where fresh breeze blew. The expansion of knowledge near fresh water is another example of Jupiter exaltation in Cancer.

Jupiter gets debilitated in Capricorn at 5 degrees; a sign ruled by Saturn. Capricorn is a sign of a high level of control, restrictions, and limitations. Therefore, the planet of expansion, feels completely hapless in this sign. The debilitated Jupiter in the horoscope shows that the person wants to do a lot in his life, but he has to face the problem of lack of resources.

5.4 Jupiter is The Protector

The highest benefic planet always provides its shield of protection to every person. With his blessings, the activities of expansion continue and life gathers momentum. When Jupiter removes its protective shield, it becomes difficult for a person to fight the negativities in life.

Jupiter is an asset that everyone wants to accumulate and feel confident having more of it in their portfolio. If Jupiter is not strong, the person soon becomes disheartened and unable to fight the difficulties of life. Remember, in the solar system Saturn comes after Jupiter who is ready to give trouble anytime. It is the shield of Jupiter which always protects us. In fact, it is our good deeds (Karma) that always protect us.

5.5 Jupiter Represents Gold

Jupiter is the lord of gold, so people collect gold, in fact, people collect Jupiter. In case of any inauspicious event in life, they want protection and want to convert inauspicious into auspicious with their accumulated wealth. Without the help of Jupiter, we cannot go away from the inauspicious. People love to wear gold and they want Jupiter to always protect them from any negativity in life.

But this is only the physical aspect and some wise people know that the collection of gold cannot last long and by adopting this method they can never attain supreme knowledge. Therefore, they seek the blessings of Jupiter to become a wise person. He who is in search of knowledge is also gathering Jupiter and wants to protect himself from the illusions of this material world. He knows that gold will slip out of his hand but wisdom does not, so he collects the subtle things of Jupiter. Jupiter represents honesty, so the first step in becoming a wise person is to be honest.

Those who collect gold, those who collect knowledge, and those who selflessly save the lives of others, are all increasing their wealth and that is Jupiter. All of them are the protective shield of Jupiter but everyone's goal is different.

5.6 Jupiter Protects from Accident

Jupiter always protects a person's life and avoids accidents. The aspect of Jupiter on the ascendant indicates that the person will recover soon from illness. The energy of Jupiter always acts as a shield and keeps the person in a safe zone from any possible harm. So, one should always help others and get involved in saving lives selflessly to make one's Jupiter strong.

Jupiter in the 6th house protects the person from any kind of inauspicious events in daily life. Jupiter in the 8th house prevents the person from any sudden accident. Jupiter in the 12th house always prevents the person from any loss including the loss of life.

5.7 Jupiter Represents Husband in a Female Chart

In the female chart, Jupiter represents the husband. An afflicted Jupiter indicates a problem in marriage and unhappy married life. Jupiter represents gold and women are fond of gold. She wants to wear gold jewelry and is very happy when her husband presents her. Jupiter means protection and every woman wants her husband to always protect her. Wearing jewelry signifies that she wants Jupiter to always protect her. People like to wear gold chains and ring as they seek the blessings of Jupiter and like to wear his protective shield.

We shouldn't make the mistake of considering Mars in the female horoscope as the husband, because Mars is considered a significator of boyfriend or a short-term partner or a passionate lover.

5.8 Jupiter and Food

The food which we eat impact the strength of the planet, and by eating such food we can strengthen its position. Jupiter represents food especially yellow food like; Yellow Pulses, Yellow Rice, Besan, Chana dal, Turmeric, and Vegetables. Jupiter rules fatty and sweet items like, Ghee, Sweets, Nuts, Seeds. Person influenced with Jupiter like to drink and eat herbal foods, tonic foods, nutritional and easy to digest sattvic vegetarian foods which helps in building body and purify blood.

It is food and water, which we absorb and that provide energy for our day-to-day life. By controlling our diet, a person can balance the energy of the planet according to his horoscope and boost the energy of the weaker planet.

5.9 Jupiter as a Counsellor

Jupiter is considered to be the Guru (Master). The planet of expansion reflects the generosity of the person. Being Dev Guru, one should always respect Jupiter. In the same manner, a person having strong Jupiter attracts respect from others. Jupiter provides knowledge and wisdom and shows the light when a person finds himself at crossroads.

Jupiter is considered a counsellor and represents all counselling activities. A strong Jupiter indicates a very honest person. Such a person is magnanimous, broad-minded, dutiful, and respects law and religion. Such a person works on making the atmosphere congenial and does not believe in any type of quarrel or fight. He believes in cooperation, works on a strategy, and waits for the outcome patiently.

5.10 Jupiter represents Freedom and Generosity

The element of Jupiter is sky, which means no limit. Hence, Jupiter represents freedom. Ignorance is slavery, knowledge is freedom. With the grace of Jupiter, a person becomes knowledgeable and wise and becomes free from all types of slavery. A positive Jupiter makes the person generous and benevolent. He is charitable and becomes a respectable member of society due to his good deeds.

Our soul is a slave to this physical body, and Lord Jupiter provides ultimate wisdom, by which one can get rid of all the miseries of human life. Our ancient texts state such a state of mind is known as "Parmanand".

5.11 Jupiter Represents Our Luck

Jupiter is our luck. Therefore, when going to do an act when the outcome is unknown, people say, "Best of luck" and seek the blessings of Lord Brihaspati. Jupiter represents the person who follows principles and does not deviate from the chosen path. Materialistic desire does not allure the person, he prefers to face any situation in life but does not ready to surrender his respect.

Physicians write "Rx" at the top of the prescription before writing their medical advice and seek the blessings of Jupiter. Rx is the Latin symbol for the planet Jupiter. Medical astrology states that taking medicine in Jupiter Hora is more beneficial than at any other time.

5.12 Jupiter is Future

Jupiter is karaka of the 5th house and this house represents creativity. Our children are our creation, and Jupiter blesses the couple with children. When a couple has a child, various necessities of the child start and they take interest in the fulfillment of all these activities, representing the expansion of life in this mundane world. Children are our future; therefore, Jupiter represents our future.

5.13 Jupiter Represents Large Organizations

The biggest planet in the solar system represents large organizations and their activities. In two decades of my career, I worked with many companies and got a chance to visit many companies' premises. During these periods some companies become very big and some are closed. I studied many companies' balance sheets and financial statements, and read and write many things related to financial and business points of view.

When I started learning astrology, I found that planetary influence is not only related to individuals, but it also affects company culture. A strong Jupiter indicates a positive culture while a weak Jupiter indicates a poor culture of the organization.

Below are some points which I observed in my career for weak and inauspicious Jupiter in the organization:

- An intelligent and talented person (Jupiter and Mercury) has no value in the organization and flatterers and sycophants (Rahu) are being promoted.

- Talented persons are forced to work under sycophants (Rahu). Jupiter and Rahu are enemies, and Jupiter can never work below Rahu, so such a person prefers to leave the organization.

- Top management takes interest only in their luxury. (Rahu starts entering the organization and slowly starts replacing Jupiter)

- Incompetent seniors, who are unable to provide any guidance to their team members. (Only Jupiter can provide direction)

- Bad food quality and no one is taking care of that even after multiple complaints. (Jupiter indicates quality and sattvic food)

The above points indicate that Jupiter is gradually moving out of such an establishment, and it will be difficult for it to exist for a long time because Jupiter is life. When debt is increasing and profitability is decreasing of a company and top management is unable to implement good strategies (only Jupiter can make good strategies), they prefer to fire their competent employees rather than reduce expenditure on their luxuries. (Rahu does not want to compromise with his comfort).

Slowly, Jupiter starts moving out from such an organization. Only Jupiter can provide the right direction, and when Jupiter is absent, people make wrong decisions. When decisions start going wrong, they become angry and eccentric. (The influence of Rahu begins to increase in the organization, and instability starts to emerge because Rahu destabilizes things.)

Gradually the pace of work starts slowing down and after some time everything starts to cool down and the legal process for liquidation of the company begins. Cold planet Saturn enters slowly and freezes everything. Rahu and Saturn are very close to each other, and Saturn uses Rahu as his agent. Where Rahu comes, Saturn's entry is certain after some time. For example, Rahu gives alcohol and smoke and Saturn gives death. Rahu gives illegal activities and Saturn gives imprisonment. Rahu gives greed and Saturn gives poverty.

Remember the ancient sutra, "Shanivat Rahu and Kujavat Ketu," i.e. in giving effect Rahu is similar to Saturn and Ketu is similar to Mars. The entry of Rahu invites Saturn. (Readers can find articles on this topic in my books "Vedic Astrology: The Light of Wisdom" or "Rahu & Ketu: The Invisible and Mysterious Planets.")

5.14 A Strong Jupiter Indicates

Jupiter provides education, and interest in religion, spiritual rhymes, philosophy, astrology, and law. A strong Jupiter indicates concentration, meditation, reading habits, thirst for knowledge, benevolence, prudent behaviour, ethics, morals, etc. Jupiter represents abundance, when it is favourable, opportunity knocks on your door. A person having strong Jupiter in his chart never breaches anyone's trust. The person will always show respect to others, favour doing the right things, and follow the path of justice. A strong Jupiter indicates that the person is never disappointed in difficult times in life and can pass such a phase with a smile. When Jupiter is weak, such a person loses hope in difficult times soon and easily falls prey to his greed.

Jupiter always prevents the native from difficulties as long as the native follow the righteous path in his life. The person will be protected by Jupiter at the last moment in a state of difficulty when every possible hope is over. A guru teaches lessons to his students and provides his guidance and protection as long as the student follows the guru's advice, but when the student stops listening to the guru after several warnings, the guru simply removes his protective shield. This is the way Jupiter works. He quietly leaves life without saying a word.

5.15 When Jupiter Becomes Malefic

Jupiter represents a person who fulfills his promises and never breaches anyone's trust. If a person does against this then Jupiter removes their shield of protection.

Jupiter punishes the person but not like Mars. Mars's attack is direct and sharp but Jupiter simply goes away without saying anything. When Jupiter becomes malefic, he removes his protection shield and stops giving direction. Without direction, the person wanders here and there and wastes his time and energy. Due to the absence of Jupiter, the direction fades away from the person's life and his futile wandering starts without any result. For example, if the disciples do not listen even after a warning, then the Master leaves the disciple, and he becomes directionless.

The darkness of ignorance gradually submerges the person. The afflicted Jupiter makes the person extreme and fanatic. It puts the person in the ocean of darkness and in the absence of knowledge, the person is not ready to listen to anyone. Because of his arrogant nature, he wanders here and there without any fruit.

Afflicted Jupiter indicates false optimism, false faith, and orthodox beliefs. A weak Jupiter indicates, a lack of hope, absence of knowledge but the belief of knowing everything, greed, materialistic nature, extravagant, overconfident, laziness, worthless promises, etc.

Such a person often uses index finger to show the direction (wrong direction) to others. The native will not be a liberal person, instead of being dutiful he will be careless and show false reputation to others. He will stay away from religious activities, and chanting spiritual rhymes are very difficult for him. He will always do improper judgments, always regret them and make mistakes in calculations.

5.16 Jupiter is the Only Asset

Jupiter is the real wealth that should be worked hard to accumulate. As this wealth of yours grows, the planet of abundance begins to open up many areas in our life.

Jupiter tends to expand the life of the person and such a person is never afraid to venture into uncharted territory. Because the unknown is a danger and without the wealth of Jupiter such a person can't dare to move forward. With this wealth, a person is ready to face any situation in life and always finds a way out, and never gets disheartened, as he has strong Jupiter in his portfolio.

When Jupiter is auspicious, the person will be protected at the last moment in a state of difficulty when every possible hope is over.

Chapter 6

Jupiter In Different Signs

The most auspicious planet stays in a zodiac sign for about a year. With his blessings the activities of expansion continue in the world, one overcomes ignorance and darkness and attains knowledge and wealth. Jupiter blesses the person with plentiful resources. Due to his blessings, one can elevate one's activities in the mundane world and lead a spiritual life at a higher level.

There are four elements and twelve signs and the behavior of Jupiter is not the same in each element and every zodiac sign.

6.1 Jupiter In the Elements

6.1.1 Fire

Fire represents energy, passion, courage, action, and the strength to overcome obstacles. On the path of spirituality, a person must be honest and have strong courage to enter the unknown world.

The planet of spirituality and honesty feels comfortable in these signs. Jupiter bestows many positive qualities on the person. Such a person is active and enthusiastic. He is kind and helpful. He has keen insight and can assess the risks involved.

Jupiter in the fire sign represents such a person will do any task if you request humbly but they don't like anyone's authoritarian nature. They are very loyal, and trustworthy and never cheat anyone.

It should be remembered that the fire sign also reflects the impulsive, aggressive and belligerent nature of a person. Therefore, these qualities are also present in a person. However, the intensity of such qualities depends on the total weightage of all the elements (count the number of planets placed in each element).

6.1.2 Earth

The earth sign represents a stable, practical, and grounded approach. The earth sign represents a firm, trustworthy and cautious person. Fire signs mean impulsive nature but earth sign means the person will act only after full consideration and patiently wait for the outcome.

Fire sign will jump into taking risks, but Earth sign's person do not engage in these activities. They do not take any step without considering all the pros and cons. The earth sign represents a person who likes to preserve things and the presence of Jupiter indicates books and other materials related to knowledge and wisdom. Such a person fully understands his responsibilities and is a highly dedicated person.

The earth sign represents materialistic desire. More planets in the earth sign indicates that such a person prefers materialism and he like to spend on the finest things in life. Jupiter in the earth sign makes the person a perfectionist and they do not accept anything below the quality level. The planets present in the earth sign indicate that the person is hardworking and Jupiter indicates that the person will work hard in acquiring knowledge. They work hard for their desired goal and their labor compares to none.

6.1.3 Air

Out of the four elements, air is elusive and it spreads fast. Jupiter is also a gaseous planet. It makes these signs extremely intelligent and their ideas are beyond imagination. They have the power to think fast, think deeply and think precisely. They create innovative and revolutionary ideas.

They are critical thinkers; therefore, logic comes first before they take any action. Rather than taking decisions based on emotions they always look about all facts and figures and always believe in logical decisions.

Air element expands the qualities of Jupiter. Therefore, the energy is high, if this person is not involved in religious and creative activities, then the mind of such a person will be involved in negative and destructive activities. Air sign indicates that they are well versed with technology and can use or misuse such knowledge in either constructive or destructive manner. They are very good computer programmers, or, on the negative side, they can become hackers and online fraudsters, or they are people who deceive others in the name of religion and spirituality.

6.1.4 Water

Water is life, without water there is no life, life gets expansion in water. Everything gets absorbed in water quickly. Hence, Jupiter feels highly comfortable in watery signs i.e., Cancer, Scorpio and Pisces. Water signs person have strong gut feelings, deep insight and possess strong memory. They are deep observer, always eyes for detail, and never miss anything from their eyes. As water takes any shape, they are ready to adjust to any conditions.

Water is very sensitive; so, they are very sensitive and emotional person. They are courteous in nature and once they make the bondage, they are very loyal to their relationships. Water provides peace but abundance of water create havoc. So, when they get angry, they get out of control and becomes like a tsunami that engulfs everything and sets out to destroy anything.

There is no creativity without water and planet of abundance provides plentiful resources. Presence of Jupiter means such person is full with creative ideas and with the blessings of Jupiter they involve in various creative activities.

They are intense thinker, but have a problem of wavering mind and due to this they delay their decisions. They are very mysterious people and it is difficult to know what is going on in their mind like the depths of unfathomable ocean. Water is not compressible, so, they become rebellious when someone puts pressure on them, and become very determined, stubborn, and outrageous.

6.2 Jupiter in 12 Signs

6.2.1 Jupiter in Aries

The first sign of the zodiac Aries is a fiery sign, ruled by Mars. Mars is a friend of Jupiter and provides due respect to the Devguru. The placement of Jupiter in this sign indicates many positive qualities to the person.

Due to the positive sign of Mars, this energy act as a protector, and the placement of Jupiter indicates the person will take care of everyone and take the right decision in critical circumstances. Devguru has a feeling of compassion towards others and it indicates a person with a clean heart.

A positive, odd, and masculine sign indicates a high level of energy and such a person cannot sit idle and always engage in doing something unique in life. Aries is movable and the first sign of the zodiac, placement of Jupiter indicates that such a person has the great initiative quality and is always ready to learn. Aries is a barren sign that indicates lack of emotions and sometimes the behaviour of the person becomes very rude.

The first sign also represents birth and Jupiter provides direction. It indicates the person can produce new and innovative ideas. Such a person has a strong foothold towards books, education, higher learning philosophy, and spirituality, etc.

6.2.2 Jupiter in Taurus

Taurus is a fixed sign ruled by Venus. Jupiter treats Venus as his enemy while Venus has a neutral attitude toward Jupiter. On the path of spirituality, no planet is inimical to each other. Planets oppose each other only in the mundane world. Venus represents sexuality and Jupiter is knowledge and wisdom.

On the path of wisdom, one must abstain oneself from sexual activities. That is why it is said in our texts that Jupiter considers Venus as his enemy. When a person follows the path of spirituality, the energy of Venus moves upwards and supports the person in his spiritual growth. Therefore, on the higher aspect of life, both the Gurus support the person, and Jupiter in Taurus provides fruitful results.

Taurus is an even, auspicious, and feminine sign and the placement of Jupiter indicates the benevolent and generous nature of a person. Such a person is very good at communication and always ready to help others; They are passionate and very sensitive person, they are wealthy and fortunate person, they are straightforward, loyal, and trustworthy person, they are responsible and hardworking person.

They always dress with dignity and never like cheap and untidy clothes. They do every work wholeheartedly and like to cross-check. They have a strong ability to complete unfinished work and wait patiently for the result without any haste.

Jupiter in Taurus indicates a very valuable person and if an organization is ready to provide due respect and take care of their needs then they never leave such an organization. Though they are materialistic, they never cheat anyone and never take anyone else's money. They work hard to fulfill their wish, but dignity is a top priority for them.

6.2.3 Jupiter in Gemini

Mercury the planet of communication is the ruler of this sign and the presence of Jupiter indicates that the person is excellent in communication, is a quick learner, and has a sharp intellect. Gemini is an airy, sattwic, and positive sign. It is an odd, masculine, and barren sign. Jupiter is a masculine planet. So, there is no meaning of emotions to these people. They are logical thinkers and take interest in solving puzzles.

It is a shudra caste sign, hence, Jupiter doesn't feel comfortable here. Uncontrolled expansion can also be witnessed here and they can use their brain to disguise and cheat others.

They are very versatile and believe in change and Jupiter indicates that in search of knowledge, they like to visit here and there. The influence of business aspects cannot be ruled out, they are those who can mentally calculate profit and loss and can visualize both sides of the coin quickly.

They are soft-spoken and cooperative; they are good advisors and diplomats. They are extroverts and their reactions are quick and witty. They are those who never keep their mouth closed. They are very good at conversation and able to tactfully convert the matter in their favor.

Mercury means an adolescent who is eager to learn and Gemini is a dual sign. The placement of Jupiter indicates duality in the matter of the respective house. Such a person is ready to learn from the master (Jupiter) but the hidden business prospects which are running deep in his mind can't be hidden from the master. They are only interested in learning that they can use it for business prospects, business is their priority and knowledge come later. They are not interested in their spiritual growth and the master realizes that such a student is not a good student. When they start misusing the knowledge provided by the master then Jupiter starts providing their inauspicious results.

6.2.4 Jupiter in Cancer

Cancer is the 4th sign of the zodiac ruled by the Moon. The sign of Cancer represents freshwater which is highly suitable for Jupiter and gets exalted here at 5 degrees. After entering the sign, the planet which provides life and expansion finds a highly suitable place where he can easily engage in the activity of expansion. Cancer is a brahmin sign and Jupiter bestows the person with great spiritual qualities.

They are a very talented and productive person. They have strong nurturing qualities and can guide others. They are generous and tenacious people and feel strong bondage with their family and culture. With the grace of Jupiter, they are wealthy and have good money management qualities.

They have a strong memory and a powerful intuition. They are soft-spoken and sensitive people. They are highly emotional and get easily hurt like a single particle destroys the purity of water. They observe deeply, notice everything, and can't overlook any matter.

They are mysterious people, who keep everything in their chest and are not ready to open up easily. They are charitable and prefer a safe environment, a peaceful home, and a family life. They are shy and non-aggressive people and do not believe in any kind of violence. They are protective and have a great desire to nurture and grow themselves and others.

Exalted Jupiter in a chart is a blessing and such a person is very lucky in many aspects of life. Jupiter always protects the person from any mishappening in life. The protective shield of Jupiter is always available because he had made some great sacrifice in his previous birth. Such a person tends to save lives and he will never do any harm to others.

6.2.5 Jupiter in Leo

Leo is the fifth sign of the zodiac and the second fiery sign. The royal kingly sign represents commitment and Jupiter indicates such a person who never goes back to his words under any circumstances. Independence and freedom are their first choice.

They are noble and generous and have large hearts. Such a person has strong religious tendencies and a strong desire for creation. They like to join a religious organization and do preaching.

Jupiter in Leo means no one can question the integrity of such a person. They are an intelligent, hardworking, and faithful person. They are individuals of their own will and do not like any bondage. This Sun sign indicates prestige and respect but planets in this sign indicates isolation and Jupiter means inclination towards higher wisdom. They find it difficult to socialize with other people and have fewer friends and social connections. They have a strong guardianship nature and take care of every individual.

They have a strong intuition which gives them a competitive advantage to make the right decisions in critical situations. They are always ready to learn and able to break down the barriers of growth. They are courageous and ready to embrace new ideas and innovations, but fixed signs indicate that they do not like to change their idealistic views and prefer to stick with their philosophies. If Jupiter is inauspicious, then such people are obstinate, over-zealous, unsocial, and take unfair decisions.

6.2.6 Jupiter in Virgo

Virgo is the 6th sign of the zodiac and is ruled by Mercury. It is a dual, earthy, and Vaishya (merchant) caste sign. Mercury represents business and trade. On the path of spirituality, there is no business, in search of truth a person cannot bargain. Jupiter doesn't like business at all, hence, it is inimical towards Mercury, but Mercury wants knowledge, so, he is neutral towards Jupiter. The planet of knowledge and wisdom in the sign of Mercury feels uncomfortable. A spiritual master does not want anyone who starts trading on the knowledge imparted by him.

Master can only provide direction but it is not his job to persevere and complete the task. Mercury represents the way to enter and complete the task. According to the instructions given by the Master, knowledge should be beneficial to all, but when Mercury starts using it for his personal gain, then Jupiter becomes malefic.

Virgo is a sattwic and negative sign. Such a person is benevolent, but it also indicates that the person can use their skills negatively to achieve what they desire. Indulgence in such activities makes

Jupiter inauspicious and the benefic planet does not give positive results in this sign.

Virgo is a feminine sign and Jupiter is a masculine planet. Here passive feminine energy is combined with active masculine energy, it shows that such a person is very good at teamwork, they are very cooperative, and always ready to help others at any time.

The planet of expansion indicates they are detail-conscious and soft-spoken people. They are a smart and active person. They are a reliable, hardworking, and stubborn person. They keep a vigil eye on every development and no one can fool them. They are a very talented person and always up-to-date with all the latest information. They believe in persistent effort, have a strong ability for creation, and do not frustrate easily by any setback.

6.2.7 Jupiter in Libra

Libra is a market place ruled by Venus. Devguru Brihaspati does not like such a place, where trading activities take place. To gather knowledge, a person has to sit at a calm and peaceful place, in the midst of the market no one can learn anything. At the market someone is shouting, someone is bargaining, people are greedy and looking for money, etc. The planet who is providing supreme knowledge and wisdom knows that this place is not suitable for such things. So, Jupiter doesn't produce fruitful results here.

Jupiter in Libra means they are polite in behaviour, etiquettes and manners are their top priorities. They always dress-up well and keep their surroundings always neat and clean. Venus is neutral to Jupiter, so they give due respect to the wise person but the market is always going on in his mind and they also see knowledge as an item to weigh.

Such person is ready to buy peace at any cost but don't want to indulge in an argument in any matter and prefer to avoid such situations in life. They listen the problem of others very carefully and always ready to help. They are showy in nature and presence of Jupiter indicates the person will show his religious tendencies to others, but his spirituality is only for ostentatious purposes.

These people cannot stay alone and like to join gatherings, ceremonies, religious sermons, etc. They love to dance and perform bhajans in temples. Having the news of any such occasion they are the first who reaches there and actively start participating in such activities.

Libra represents balance; therefore, Saturn gets exalted here. But Jupiter nature is not to do balance, the planet of abundance creates imbalance in this sign due to excessive involvement in external activities and can create chaos in the matter related to the concerned house.

6.2.8 Jupiter in Scorpio

Scorpio is the 8th sign of the zodiac and ruled by Mars. This sign is the most mysterious part of the zodiac where everything is under deep cover. Scorpios' are very good in search and investigation. It is a brahmin caste, feminine, and even sign. Presence of Jupiter indicates search in the field of occult and spirituality. They have strong power to penetrate and find the hidden truth. But it is a negative and tamasic sign, that indicates that the person may misuse of their knowledge and power. They may misuse their occult knowledge and can become a black magician.

They have strong capacity to understand the human mind and able to see behind the scenes. In search of truth they can enter into any well, take dive into any ocean and until they find the truth, they cannot take rest. They can expand their search up to any extent until they unfold the mystery, their nights are sleepless.

They have tendency to hide everything and placement of Jupiter indicates they do not share their knowledge with anyone. Scorpio is a fixed sign, when water is fixed at one place it starts going down. The planet of expansion, indicates they can go up to any beneath, underneath the surface and find the hidden things. But when water remains stagnant at one place for a long time, it becomes muddy. Scorpio water is muddy, so, they do not trust anyone easily. All their actions are in deep silence and they are highly unpredictable person.

This is the sign of transformation and placement of Jupiter indicates transformation at higher level. They work as a healer and they are those who protect the person from the poison. They suggest good medicine to others and can-do fine surgery.

They don't share their opinion and they are hard believer of their ideologies. Their memory is very strong and can work for hours. They are very stubborn and don't like a question on their opinion. They have strong fighting spirit and not ready to compromise under any circumstances.

On the higher aspects, the continuous fighting spirit represents till the attainment of "The Ultimate Truth" they will not surrender. The presence of Jupiter means they have strong energy for spiritual growth.

6.2.9 Jupiter in Sagittarius

Sagittarius is the 9th sign of the zodiac and the third fiery sign. It is a positive sign of Jupiter and also its Mooltrikona Sign. A positive sign represents the masculine qualities of Jupiter, so they are ambitious and dauntless people. It indicates a high level of religious tendencies, but on the negative side, it represents fanatics. They are wanderers and the placement of Jupiter indicates wandering to religious places and for religious matters.

Sagittarius means to explore the unknown and the quest for knowledge and truth. Such a person has a strong tendency to explore the unknown world and find the truth, they are even ready to burn their fingers but are unwilling to step back. The planet of expansion bestows the person with many positive qualities and is full of innovative ideas but over-expansion could become a problem.

The presence of Jupiter represents the truthfulness of the person. Being Kshatriya (warrior) caste sign they are ready to fight for justice. An odd, fierce, and fire sign indicates harsh tendencies and they speak harsh truth without hesitation. Sagittarius represents transformation and the placement of Jupiter represents the transformation of the person in the latter half of life. But any transformation is not easy, therefore, such a person's life is not smooth and he has to witness many changes. The symbol of Sagittarius is half-horse and half-man. So, along with Jupiter if more planets are placed here, then the person has to face multiple challenges in life and every challenge makes them stronger.

6.2.10 Jupiter in Capricorn

Capricorn is the 10th sign of the zodiac and is ruled by Saturn. Jupiter gets debilitated in this sign at 5 degrees. This earthy sign keeps everything in full control. The planet of expansion feels highly misfit in this sign because Capricorn puts control and restrictions on everything and does not allow Jupiter to move. We can say that the sky is under control in Capricorn. Therefore, after entering this sign Jupiter feels highly uncomfortable and gets debilitated. It means such a person has to face the lack of resources in his life, he has a great desire for expansion but he moves only inch by inch.

Due to the effect of Saturn, they don't like to mingle with people and prefer aloofness in life. The presence of Jupiter indicates morality and discipline are at the highest level. Jupiter and Saturn are neutral towards each other. Discipline is required in the path of spirituality so that a person can easily follow such a path in life.

Capricorn is represented by the sea-goat, a mythological creature with the body of a goat and the tail of a fish. The first half of the sign is quadruped and the second half is footless. The first 15 degrees are non-movable and the second 15 degrees have a tail that represents movement. When Jupiter is placed in the first 15 degrees of the sign, then such a person faces too many restrictions in his life. It makes a person a strict ideologist who is not ready to compromise under any circumstances. Once they decide, then it is very difficult to change it.

When Jupiter is in the second half of Capricorn, movement is witnessed and activity increases. Such a person listens to the advice of others and take decisions as per the circumstances.

They always discuss rationally. Their approach is very practical and very good at planning. They are good at investigation, are not satisfied after superficial observation, and want to delve deeper into the matter. They have a strong ability to take the right decisions and their decisions rarely go wrong.

Capricorn means uses at the highest level. Jupiter in Capricorn means that the person has a good and unique collection of rare things. Although the resources are limited, they have a strong ability to overcome all the difficulties.

6.2.11 Jupiter in Aquarius

The lord of Aquarius is Saturn which is neutral towards Jupiter. The Aquarius symbol is a man pouring a water pot which shows the strong relation of water with this sign. Jupiter bestows the person with various humanitarian qualities. But Aquarius is a tamasic and shudra caste sign, so, Jupiter is not very comfortable here and does not produce good results. The placement of Jupiter indicates they are silent and hardworking and don't like to show their work to others. They don't want interference from others and don't allow any person to enter their circle. They prefer long-lasting relationships but stick to their principles.

They have patience and believe in perseverance. They have excellent problem-solving skills, deep thinkers, and can read the hidden motive of others. They are a very practical and intelligent person who uses such energy for the upliftment of others. It is a fixed sign and the presence of Jupiter indicates they don't go back to their words. They are a very intuitive person and have strong retention power.

Co-rulership of Uranus indicates sudden changes and the presence of Jupiter means such a person develops religious tendencies after a setback or some incident in life.

6.2.12 Jupiter in Pisces

Pisces is a watery sign ruled by Jupiter. It is a brahmin caste sign and the quality of the sign is Moksha. They are philosophical and always thirsty for knowledge. They are very honest and wise people. They are kind and loyal people. Due to a feminine sign, they are very polite and non-combative. They easily forgive people for their mistakes.

They are highly responsible people and never leave any work in the middle or anyone in the lurch. They have a sharp memory and pay full attention to completing the task before taking on any new assignment. To gain knowledge one should be very receptive and should give up ego and Jupiter in this sign gives such qualities to the person.

They are very generous and ready to share their knowledge with others. They are the great master and their teachings are very different. Students love to attend the class of such a teacher and they also gain popularity among the students.

Pisces represents ocean water and Jupiter is a gaseous planet that represents fog and mist. If it is afflicted, they are indecisive, always in dilemma, and unable to take a concrete decision. It also represents illusionary and daydreamers who are away from reality.

On the higher aspects, Jupiter in Pisces produces a very creative personality and a great artist. They learn astrology and other occult sciences and get immersed in the ocean of spirituality.

Chapter 7

Jupiter In Different Houses

Astrology has divided the 360-degree space into 12 equal sections known as Houses or Bhavas (in Sanskrit). These 12 houses denote the different aspects of human life. Behind the houses, there are zodiac signs, and the transit of planets continuously affects such energy. Therefore, for interpretation of a horoscope understanding of four things are very important, the meaning of the signs, the meaning of the houses, the placement of planets and effect of transit.

All activities of human life are reflected by these 12 houses. The ascendant is very important because it denotes the structure of the human body. The zodiac sign moves one after the other towards the horizon, changing every two hours and rising again in the east about 24 hours later. The sign in the ascendant and the placement of the planets plays an important role in deciding the physical structure of the person.

Jupiter is known as the most beneficial planet. It is the planet of expansion and space. But there are some negativities also associated with them. The presence of Jupiter in a house not only gives positive results but also negative ones. Where the activity of expansion is involved, it should be controlled, otherwise, it will create multiple problems in the life of the person. For example, as excessive consumption of sugar can alter the taste buds.

The infinite expansion means "God". Therefore, Hindu astrology says that the higher aspect of Jupiter is "Lord Vishnu". To please Jupiter, one must always worship "Lord Vishnu".

7.1 Jupiter In The First House

The zodiac sign rising on the eastern horizon at the time of the birth of the person comes under the ascendant. Such a person is very lucky when Jupiter is placed in the first house of his horoscope. Jupiter bestows the person with a nice and attractive physical body. Such a person is good-looking, generous, wise, wealthy, and benevolent. He is a very honest and characterful person, never makes false promises, and always keeps his word. They are a broad-minded, knowledgeable, and spiritual person. They are philosophical and take an interest in religious activities.

From here, Jupiter aspects the 5th house, the 7th house, and the 9th house. The 5th house is the house of children and creativity. The 7th house is the house of the spouse and the 9th is the house of Bhagya (luck). With the blessings of Lord Jupiter, such a person is very happy in all these aspects of life.

The first house represents the life span and Jupiter bestows the person with a long life. The first house represents the head and the brain and Jupiter always protects the person from any injury to his head. The protective shield of Jupiter is always available with the person when it is placed in the ascendant. They are never alone when it comes to any bad situation in life, they always get help. The first house represents name, fame, dignity, self-respect, prestige, physic of the person, etc. and Jupiter provides all such things to the person.

If Jupiter is weak or in a bad position then the person can be gullible, overly emotional, extravagant, and take a wrong decision. His body can be bulky and he may have diseases related to Jupiter.

7.2 Jupiter In The Second House

Jupiter in the second house provides an expansion to the family, possessions, and savings. Plenty of wealth is available in water and on earth. If Jupiter is placed in any watery or earthy sign in this house then it indicates a wealthy person. Jupiter in the second house also indicates having a large family. Such a person is soft-spoken and very good at communication. They are very generous and charitable. They lead a luxurious life and are fond of tasty food.

The quality of Jupiter is expansion and if it is not controlled then it creates problems for the native. Such a person may have an uncontrollable desire to become super rich and his interest becomes more in savings. He likes to eat fatty foods and may have heart attack problems. This is the reason our text says Jupiter gives inauspicious results where it is placed.

The second house represents the right eye, nose, mouth, nails, and teeth of the native. An inauspicious Jupiter indicates problems in these parts of the body.

It must be remembered that the planetary energy always moves in a geometric shape and the second, sixth and tenth houses are the 'Earth Triangle Houses'. Earth means wealth which cannot be obtained without doing an action (Karma). Hence, to understand the financial situation of a person, one should not focus only on the second house, but it is necessary to consider all the earth's triangular houses along with the study of Navamsha kundali.

From here, Jupiter's 5th aspect is on the 6th house, 7th aspect is on the 8th house and 9th aspect is on the 10th house. Jupiter protect the person from enemies, he take interest in occult activities and do a respected job in his life.

7.3 Jupiter In The Third House

Third house is the house of courage and ruler of this house is Mars. This is the house of expression and communication and Jupiter provides good communication skills. Such a person has knowledge of multiple languages and able to express his ideas profoundly. This is the house of letters and documents, writing and publishing. Jupiter indicates that such a person is good in writing and publishing.

The third house is the 'Marna Karak Sthan' (Feels like dying) for Jupiter and he feels uncomfortable in the house of Mars. It is the home of siblings - especially of younger brothers and sisters, cousins, neighbours, casual acquaintances and indicates a relationship to them. Jupiter does not want to sit here, and gives negative results in any of the above aspects. It can create problems in relations towards siblings and Mars indicates quarrel.

Due to benevolent nature such a person will sacrifice a lot towards his brothers and sisters, but they will not give them any respect. They will immediately forget all the help and sacrifices made by him and will be ready to quarrel with him over any trivial matter. Such person may be a respectable person in the society due to his writing and communication skills but for his siblings he is only a cash cow. As long as they are in need, they will give artificial respect, when the meaning is gone the person will be forgotten forever.

The sloka "Sthana Hani Karo Jeeva" does not mean Jupiter will destroy all the fruitful results of that house. Jupiter in this house gives loss of "respect" from siblings.

From here, Jupiter's 5th aspect is on the 7th house, 7th aspect is on the 9th house and 9th aspect is on the 11th house. Such a person makes good relation with his partner but placement of Jupiter in the 3rd house is not a very good placement. The uncomfortable Jupiter also create the matter uncomfortable, however, such a person takes care of his father and provide due respect and get some very loyal friends in his life.

7.4 Jupiter In The Fourth House

Fourth house in the natural zodiac ruled by Moon. If Jupiter is situated here in Cancer, Sagittarius or Pisces then it gives many auspicious results. Jupiter bestows the person with property and vehicles and a strong Jupiter indicates many possessions and vehicles. Fourth house indicates mother and happiness. They feel happy at home and with mother. Early years of education have a significant impact in their life, and later they lead their life peacefully.

Fourth house is the nadir point of the zodiac and it represents our emotions, sensitivity, heart, dreams, and desires. Jupiter in this house indicates a benevolent person having a large heart. The energy of Jupiter here supports for deep and pensive thinking. Such a person is very helpful at his work place and his dreams are big. If 10th lord is situated in the fourth house, then they prefer to work from home and Jupiter indicates a big and peaceful home. Such people live at a place where office and home are together or create a space at their home for his office.

The fourth, eighth and twelfth houses form a triangle and there the elements are the same. The 8th house represents occult and the 12th house represents moksha. A strong Jupiter indicates, such a person has deep interest towards occult sciences and spend more time in search of truth in later years of his life. If the planets in these houses are very strong then they become spiritual masters.

The water sign on the fourth house indicates a high level of sensitivity, emotions and the fourth house also represent our heart. Therefore, water, emotions and heart means, although they are very cheerful in nature but they cry very easily and are unable to bear the difficult and shocking news in life. When Jupiter is situated in any watery sign in the 4th house then it is good not to tell any unwanted news suddenly to such a person which they cannot bear because of their emotional involvement. Jupiter in 4th house is not good for heart. From this point of view the planet giving abundance and highest benefic results gives negative results here.

From here, Jupiter's 5th aspect is on the 8th house, 7th aspect is on the 10th house and 9th aspect is on the 12th house. Such a person is interested in secret knowledge, does prestigious work and spends on religious subjects and secret knowledge.

7.5 Jupiter In The Fifth House

The presence of Jupiter in the fifth house indicates the wise, generous, and kind nature of the person. Such a person learns quickly and has a strong knowledge of ancient texts. He respects his tradition and can be a good mentor. The planets in this house indicate a change in job or profession and Jupiter indicates that one's natural inclination is always to learn something along with work.

The fifth house is known as the "Purva Punya Sthan", i.e., the good deeds of our past lives, Jupiter indicates that the person has a strong inclination towards mantras, worship, and religion. Our creativity is nothing but the accumulation of our karma. Jupiter indicates creativity towards knowledge and such a person can become a good writer and a preacher.

It is the house of our creativity and Jupiter is the Karaka of this house. Children are our creation and with the blessing of Jupiter person gets healthy and talented children. The children of such a person can be proficient in some art or specific field and can be very successful in life. It is the home of entertainment and romance; With the presence of the Jupiter, such a person is fond of books and prefer company of only knowledgeable person, for them entertainment, romance and knowledge all are co-related.

In this house, if Jupiter is posited in a fruitful sign (Cancer, Scorpio, and Pisces) it indicates creativity at a high level, while a semi-fruitful sign (Taurus, Libra, Sagittarius, Capricorn, Aquarius) indicates some struggle and a barren sign (Aries, Gemini, Leo, and Virgo) indicates the problem and the person gets success after persistent efforts.

From this house Jupiter aspect, the 9th house, the 11th house, and the ascendant. The aspect on the 9th house makes the native lucky, the aspect on the 11th house indicates a good source of income, and knowledgeable friends, aspect on the ascendant provides long life.

It is a house of speculation and gambling. When afflicted, the planet of expansion indicates big bets and wrong decisions. Even a very intelligent person may lose everything and all his expansion activities may fail if he takes wrong decisions and is unable to control the expansion.

Too busy with work is also not good, as it indicates that one may miss out on various other important things in life. Recall the puranic story, of how Brihaspati lost his wife Tara because of his busyness in the court of Devraj Indra.

Jupiter in the 5th house is very auspicious and bestows many virtues, but one can lose his most valuable things due to his excessive busyness and the most beneficial planet gives negative results due to not taking the right decision at proper time and situation.

7.6 Jupiter In The Sixth House

When Jupiter is situated in the sixth house, the behavior of such a person is very cordial and they never fight at the workplace. They are an honest and loyal person. They always give due respect to others. It is the house of discipline and Jupiter indicates that one will follow the noble path.

The planet of spirituality feels uncomfortable here as it is an earth triangle and its Karaka is Mars. Therefore, the pleasant situation does not remain the same and many ups and downs are witnessed with their health and daily routine. This is the house of wounds and accidents and Jupiter always protects the person.

From this place, Jupiter's 5th aspect is on the 10th house, the 7th aspect is on the 12th house and the 9th aspect is on the 2nd house. Jupiter support comes at the workplace and helps the person to increase savings. A strong 6th house indicates the person will overpower his enemies and will keep under control his subordinates. The faithfulness of juniors is also ascertained from this house, they will listen, respect, and obey the master if a strong Jupiter is situated here.

The person has a strong immune system and has protection from diseases. It is the house of the abdomen. They are very peculiar in eating and like to eat rich and tasty foods. Always eating rich food can upset the abdomen and the immunity system may get affected.

The sixth house is both; the Upachaya house and the Dusthana house. The planets placed in this house provide growth in life but also give difficulties. For example, a person gets a promotion but also gets transferred to another city. The position of Jupiter helps in the growth of the individual but overindulgence in activities can create problems. Any planet in the second house will help you in your growth but difficulties will also come. When such a person does not control his activities or is over-indulged in some work, the auspicious planet gives negative results and there may be problems in the liver, intestine, and blood circulation.

7.7 Jupiter In The Seventh House

It is the house of marriage and partnership and Jupiter indicates a faithful and trustworthy partner. When such a person looks for a partner or business partner, they are interested in building a long-term relationship and take care to nurture that relationship. Due to the influence of Jupiter, they never cheat their partner and such relationships bring fruitful results for them. The spouse of such a person is very lucky and can see an increase in fortune after marriage.

Such a person is very good at negotiation and when Jupiter is situated in any of the Mercurian signs (Gemini and Virgo), then such a person is a hard core negotiator and has strong business acumen. They are very good mediators; they are the ones who settle the conflicts of others.

From here the fifth aspect of Jupiter is on the 11th house which is the house of income; The 7th aspect is on Lagna which provides protection, and the 9th aspect is on the 3rd house which is the house of siblings. The positive effect of Jupiter can be seen here.

However, the 7th house is not a good placement for Jupiter because it gets directional weakness here. Jupiter gives expansion where it is placed and here it indicates that they look for a fully loyal partner including business partners and their expectations are very high.

When Jupiter is placed with malefic or aspects by them then the person becomes skeptical and starts distrusting his partner instead of trusting him. Such a person craves complete loyalty and attention and cannot tolerate deviations of any kind. They start questioning and doubting every action. They do not trust their partners at all and they are the ones who spy on their partners. In this house, Jupiter gives a loss of 'Trust'.

7.8 Jupiter In The Eighth House

The eighth house is the most mysterious house of the zodiac and deals with all the secret matters of life. Jupiter indicates that the native will take interest in secret matters and will work for research and investigation. They work hard to solve the mystery and can go to any extent to find the truth. It is a house of debt, and Jupiter indicates they can get loans easily. Being readily available, sometimes they take too many loans and its repayment becomes a problem for them.

Eighth House indicates everything dark and hidden, it indicates a secret room and such a person prefers to sit alone in his room, hide all activities and away from rest of the world. In this sign, Jupiter points to the knowledge-related things scattered here and there in the room and the person is engaged only in solving the mystery. Jupiter indicates life; it means that the person will seek to heal something for mankind. A strong Jupiter indicates financial gains through marriage and inheritance.

This is the house of transformation and longevity but no change is easy. Jupiter indicates a change towards religion and spirituality and bestows the person with a long life. This is the house of sudden events and unexpected gains and Jupiter indicates positivity on these fronts.

The eighth house is the darkest place in the zodiac. Jupiter provides a plethora of activities in the dark and such a person like to do research and other work at night. They are the ones who can go to any extent to find the roots of the problem. Such a person takes a keen interest in esoteric science and has strong intuitive abilities. Sometimes they behave like a psychic, being more involved in mystery. Jupiter in the 8th house means that such a person does not care about his social image at all. Planets in the 8th house indicates such a person don't care for taboos and never pay attention to what others have to say.

From here, Jupiter's 5th aspect is on the 12th house which is the house of expenses, the 7th aspect is on the 2nd house which is the house of family and savings, and the 9th aspect is on the 4th house which is the house of home and happiness. Such a person does not listen to anyone's advice in the matter of expenditure, he is extravagant and do secret expenses. Jupiter bestow the person with family, savings and home. The native takes a liberal approach in family matters, gives freedom to everyone and is busy in his secret activities.

7.9 Jupiter In The Ninth House

It is the house of fortune and Jupiter means good fortune. It bestows the person many positive qualities; He is a broad-minded, kind, benevolent, optimistic, and wise person. He takes a deep interest in philosophy and possesses strong knowledge of law and religion. It is the house of the father and Jupiter indicates a knowledgeable and respectable father in society.

This is the house of higher learning, experts, advisors, masters, long journeys, and foreign affairs. Strong Jupiter indicates a scholar with many degrees. Jupiter provides direction, and placement in its own house means such a person has a strong ability to guide others. They work as a teacher, a preacher, and a master. They take long journeys in life and in search of knowledge they prefer to travel anywhere in the world.

When Jupiter is afflicted, a person becomes a strong believer in his religion only and does not listen to the thoughts and opinions of others. They take pride in their knowledge and instead of learning they like to impose their ideas and laws on others.

Such a person becomes orthodox. They don't learn anything new and consider their thoughts and beliefs supreme. They become blind followers, unwilling to listen to anyone and believe that they are always right.

On the negative side, Jupiter in the ninth house makes a fanatic. Such a person does not hesitate to commit any crime in the name of his faith, tradition, and religion.

From here, Jupiter's 5th aspect is on the 1st house, 7th aspect is on the 3rd house and 9th aspect is on the 5th house. It is a good placement of Jupiter and the planet of benevolence protect the person from all the matters related to these houses.

7.10 Jupiter In The Tenth House

It is the house of karma, it represents our profession, the source of livelihood, and the nature of work. Jupiter indicates a successful career with literary pursuits. Such a person can easily get a job. The profession includes; Teaching, Banking, Financial Advisor, Publications, Government Advisor, Minister, Head of Department, Priest, etc. Jupiter makes a person very honest, loyal, and responsible at the workplace. They are highly dedicated people and work is worship for them.

The 10th house is the highest point of the zodiac known as Medium Coeli or Midheaven (MC). Hence, actions and anomalies associated with the house are highly visible. They work in an important position and their actions are easily noticed. When Mahadasha and antardasha of Jupiter come, the career of a person shines. The placement of Jupiter in this house makes a person wealthy, it provides a peaceful home and a pleasant and cordial workplace.

The tenth house on body parts represents the knee, which supports the movement and ability to handle pressure. Jupiter indicates that they have a strong ability to handle work pressure and do not get frustrated easily.

On the downside, such a person may face work-life balance problems in life. Jupiter expands the workplace and creates imbalance in other aspects of life.

From here, Jupiter's 5th aspect is on the 2nd house, 7th aspect is on the 4th house and 9th aspect is on the 6th house. Such a person is efficient in saving, leads a happy life and gets security in daily life.

7.11 Jupiter In The Eleventh House

The 3rd, 6th, 10th, and 11th houses are known as Upachaya houses; The planets located here provide acceleration in the life of the native. The Eleventh House is the house of income, desires, wishes, and hopes. Jupiter helps the native to achieve all the desired things in life as long as the person is kind and follows the path of benevolence. Jupiter is a benevolent planet and cannot support wrongful earnings and wrong desires. Jupiter indicates that such a person is generous and benevolent towards income and profit. Jupiter keeps hope alive even in difficult situations and the person prioritizes acquiring knowledge in his aspiration.

This is the house of attachment, affection, friends, social lives, and a network of people. They have good friends and like a knowledgeable and helpful person in their surroundings. They like to participate in religious activities. If Rahu is in the eleventh house, the person prefers to go to pubs and bars but the presence of Jupiter indicates that such a place is a temple and where religious activities are going on. Social image matters to them and they take care of it.

From here Jupiter views the third, and seventh houses, activating the triangle of the house of desires (Kama Triangle). On the higher aspect, such a desire is towards spiritualism but on the lower aspect, it is towards materialism. The seventh aspect of Jupiter is on the fifth house and the planet bestows the person with obedient children.

It is the house of excessive indulgence for material gains. The presence or aspect of malefics in this house indicates obsession towards material desire and the person turns away from spiritual path. Such a person may indulge excessively for the fulfillment of his desire and may go to any extent to achieve such a purpose and may leave all religious activities forever. When the fulfillment of the desires of the senses becomes a top priority, then the highest benefic planet starts giving negative results here.

The sloka "Sthana Hani Karo Jeeva" is right in this context and for the 11th house it is "Uncontrolled Desire".

From here, Jupiter's 5th aspect is on the 3rd house, 7th aspect is on the 5th house and 9th aspect is on the 7th house. Such a person always maintains good relations with his siblings, his children are obedient and talented and he is always caring and concerned about his life partner.

7.12 Jupiter In The Twelfth House

The twelfth house is the last house of the zodiac which signifies the journey towards the end and for every soul it is salvation. Hence, it is the house of liberation, solitude, and meditation. It is the house of expenditure and Jupiter indicates a person with spiritual tendency and who likes to spend more on religious activities.

This is the house of selfless deeds; the presence of Jupiter makes the person charitable and they are those who can give their valuable items to others without hesitation. They like to offer help to others and work as a helper at religious places. It is the house of bed pleasure but they do not take much interest and like to discuss the matter of spirituality and higher aspects of life. It is the house of foreign land and any relation with the third, fourth, eighth, ninth, or tenth house can send the person abroad. We must keep in mind that abroad does not always mean a foreign country, rather it means a change in culture.

They are liberal and extravagant and it is very difficult for them to control their expenditure. In the name of religion, they are ready to spend a lot. They like to visit religious places and do charity. They like to donate to orphanages, temples, and holy places. It is the house of prison, the presence of Jupiter or any aspect of it protects the person from going to jail.

Jupiter has supreme knowledge and that is available at the twelfth house. Hence, it is the house of liberation, and Jupiter is the lord of this house. But the path to attain such liberation is provided by Venus. Hence, Venus is exalted in this sign. It also indicates that one will sit in meditation and do spiritual practices if his Venus is strong. To get divine knowledge from Jupiter, one has to walk on the path paved by Venus. Therefore, in the lives of some people, their wife becomes their greatest teacher.

The 12th house signifies hospitals, beds, losses, and accidents. The placement of Jupiter indicates that the person will always be protected from losses and accidents. They have such a blessing that the universal force always protects them from any harm. They are the ones who always survive in an accident, they are the only survivors in a fatal accident, in a state of complete disarray they are the luckiest because Jupiter's protection shield is always available with them. It is the house of solitude and the aspect of Saturn on this house put the person in isolation in later years of life.

This house indicates conspiracy, cunningness, fraud, and deception. The presence of Jupiter indicates they never do any conspiracy with anyone, they never cheat anyone, and they never indulge in any activity of fraud and deception. One can blindly believe the loyalty of these individuals. Due to their charitable nature, they rarely demand the money given to others. But they are naive and are unable to catch the hidden motive of others. They never cheat anyone but can be easily cheated by others.

Due to their benevolent nature, such a person easily believes the things said by others. Just as a nurse is always ready to help a patient, so when they see a person in distress, they are ready to help immediately. They like to help others but do not like to differentiate between truth and falsehood and people can take advantage of his goodness. Jupiter in this house causes harm by "Being More Benevolent".

From here, Jupiter's 5th aspect is on the 4th house, 7th aspect is on the 6th house and 9th aspect is on the 8th house. Such a person feels attachment to his home and always likes to take care of his home. They get respect and cooperation at their workplace, they keep many things secret and very rarely open or open after a long time.

Chapter 8

Jupiter With Other Planets

When two or more planets are placed in the same zodiac, they affect each other. The combined energies of the planets along with the elements of the zodiac influence the matter related to the house. For example, suppose there is a 30 feet long room and only one person lives in that room, then he is responsible for all the matters related to the room. But if there are two persons located, then the first person can't decide the whole matter of the room, the decision of the second person also matters.

The relationship between these two persons is very important for the proper functioning of the house. If the relationship is friendly then both are happy and do good for the house, if the relationship is not friendly then they blame each other, don't care if something goes wrong, and don't take care of the house. If the relationship is worse, then boundaries start forming in the house as well and this worsens the matter in the person's life. If two or more planets are situated in a house then they behave in this way.

It is also necessary to see the difference between degrees among the planets. If they are enemies and are in close conjunction (less than 8 degrees) then all the energy in the house gets disturbed. One disturbed house is sufficient to create enough imbalance in the life of the native.

But when good friends live in the same room, then the atmosphere is pleasant. The posited planet knows that his friendly planet is going to support him. So, the affairs of the house flourish and life becomes easy.

Jupiter's natural tendency is to expand the affairs of the respective house. When the expanding energy mixes with different types of energies in different environments (elements), then different results occur in life. The positive qualities of a conjunction come when both the planets are firmly situated in a house and it should also not be in conjunction or aspected by malefic planets. Otherwise, negative qualities of such conjunction can also be observed in the individual.

Now, we will discuss the action and outcome of Jupiter when it conjoins with other planets. Here, it is necessary to consider that the same conjunction does not give the same results in every household. Where the planets get directional power, a conjunction becomes strong, and where planets get directional weakness a weak conjunction is formed. On the other hand, if the planets are situated in the Maran Karaka Sthan or Dusthana, then the force of the conjunction becomes weak.

8.1 Jupiter – Sun

The Sun is known as the king and Jupiter is the advisor. Therefore, this combination means the king is accompanied by his advisor. A king needs good consultation without which he cannot take proper decisions. Hence, a knowledgeable counselor is always needed by the king who provides proper guidance and the kingdom flourishes. Such a conjunction bestows the person with many positive qualities.

If the advisor does not give the right advice and the king acts on his wrong advice, then such a decision causes great harm to the state.

Both Sun and Jupiter are sattvic, fiery and masculine planets. The Sun is the supreme giver and illuminates the world. Jupiter represents generosity, wisdom, and abundance. So, this is a very good conjunction and it indicates that such a person is very pious, religious, visionary, and knowledgeable. They are optimistic, enthusiastic, and have a sense of guardianship. They can be experts in a field and provide necessary guidance to others. They work as ministers, advisors, or senior officials of the government.

The Sun is known as the Soul and Jupiter is the Jeeva (body). This conjunction indicates a lively and vibrant personality who can make necessary and right decisions. On the other hand, over-enthusiasm, supremacy, and arrogant behavior also can't be ruled out.

This conjunction is good in fire signs. A very vibrant personality is witnessed if such conjunction takes place in Aries, Leo, and Sagittarius. Jupiter feels comfortable in the water signs but Sun does not. So, they are good at counseling but their vitality is limited. They can give good advice to others but when it comes to them, then they avoid it. Earth element does not support the fire element.

So, in the earth sign, this conjunction provides limited results. The air element supports fire, so this conjunction considered to be good, but not a very good conjunction. They are intelligent but sometimes the advice of such a person is impractical and devoid of ground. Because the air expands rapidly, their ideas are out of the box, but if Jupiter is weak then acting on the thoughts of such a person can cause harm.

A strong Jupiter is necessary for a good advice. So, mere conjunction is not sufficient to analyze a horoscope. It is necessary to check the strength of the planets. In which element such conjunction is taking place and also in which nakshatra the planets are situated?

If Jupiter is situated in Ashlesha, Vishakha, or Purva Bhadrapada Nakshatra, then the advice of such a person is not a simple advice. They work in secret and there can be hidden meanings behind every action. If malefic influenced such a combination, then they could even become conspirators.

8.2 Jupiter – Moon

Jupiter provides direction and Moon represents mind, when mind gets proper direction, the result is always fruitful. Hence, it is an extremely auspicious combination and bestows the person with many positive qualities. Both Jupiter and Moon are highly beneficial planets and the conjunction of these two forms "Gajakesari Yoga". Such persons are humble, gentle and benevolent. They have a firm mind, able to provide direction and possess ability to speak well. They don't get discouraged easily and are successful in finding direction even in difficult situations. This yoga bestows a person with wealth, position, prestige as well as long life.

Moon in the fire sign indicates hot temper can't be ruled out. However, Jupiter bestows many positive qualities to the person.

In Earth signs, Moon feels comfortable as water supports earth. Moon in the earth sign indicates stubborn behaviour and Jupiter in Capricorn indicates lack of resources.

In air signs; fire and wind support each other but water does not. Therefore, the qualities of Jupiter expand here but mind never gets stable easily. Such a person is very intelligent and sharp minded people. They can think up ideas beyond the imagination. If this conjunction is in the sign of Gemini and Virgo then business comes first in their mind and if such yoga is in the seventh house, then the person is a hard negotiator.

As per astrology, Moon and Jupiter both are watery planets. Therefore, many positive qualities along with feminine tendencies are seen in the nature of the person. They are very generous and are always ready to help others. Their sensitivity is very high, they have strong intuition and can catch the hidden motives of others. On the other hand, they are very moody and unable to take concrete decisions. They are always in dilemma and often change their decisions.

8.3 Jupiter – Mars

Jupiter and Mars are friends of each other. Mars is the planet of energy and Jupiter provides direction. When energy gets direction, fruitful results are obtained. Mars represents action and without a goal, there is no meaning of action. Jupiter shows the goal and the way to use energy constructively. Such a combination bestows many positive qualities to the person. One achieves high success in the field of sports, adventure sports, police department, military, etc.

An energetic person can't sit silently. When energy is high, Martians are inclined to take risk and they do not bother about the outcome. But the person having this conjunction stops taking unnecessary risks. They have the capacity to take the right decision at the time of imminent risk. The assessment of risk of such a person is beyond the comparison of any other person. Their mind immediately captures the imminent danger and gives a signal to control the movement. On the path where others feel afraid to go, they can easily walk. They can lead others on risky projects and have the ability to climb steep and difficult mountains. Jupiter represents big plans. Hence, such conjunction provides the capability to handle riskier tasks. They are those who can handle big projects in the corporate world.

In the fire signs, this conjunction creates a highly energetic and lively personality. Therefore, such energy should be controlled and used constructively. It should not be affected by any malefic planets otherwise they may fall prey to temptation. Jupiter provides direction to achieve the goal but malefic planets can deviate the person from the chosen path.

Jupiter's energy is limited in earth's signs and Mars' energy is controlled. Here, energy is high but resources are limited, but they have a rational mind and don't get discouraged easily. The move is bound by various rules and regulations. Earthy signs represent loyalty, hard work, and devotion. This conjunction reveals such qualities in a person.

In air signs, the energy is high but it is not auspicious. They utilize such energy only for their gains. They take correct decisions but they bother only for their desire. If such conjunction forms in any Mercurian signs, then the matter of business is high but humanitarian aspects come if such conjunction forms in Aquarius.

Water signs are good for Jupiter but not for Mars. The qualities of Jupiter are high but the qualities of Mars become limited. Therefore, such a combination is not good for external activities if it formed in Cancer. But it is one of the best conjunctions as it can produce great writers, investigators, researchers etc. They can sit in one place for hours, can think deeply and have the ability to find hidden truths. If there is such a conjunction in Cancer, then the person has the quality of becoming a writer, Scorpio has the quality of being an investigator and Pisces has the quality of doing research in the medical field.

8.4 Jupiter – Mercury

Both Mercury and Jupiter are benefic planets and represent intelligence and knowledge. Hence, a person with this conjunction is known for his intelligence and wisdom. They are highly learned persons and work as professors or consultants. They are not afraid of heavy data or bundles of books. They have the power to absorb all that information quickly. They work as data scientists, programmers or in other jobs where large information is available and intelligence is needed to find results.

Mercury belongs to the Vaishya caste and represents trade and business while Jupiter represents pure wisdom which can be attained by a person only if he walks on the path of honesty and spirituality. Business and money are primary for Mercury whereas Jupiter does not always like to discuss money matters hence keeps enmity with Mercury. Such conjunction indicates that profit comes first in that person's life. For them, religion is also for profit, and they worship if there is some benefit from doing that. They are a very sharp-minded person and have no intention to harm others. They like to do charity, but it is only for the successful operation of their business.

Jupiter bestows strong judgment ability with high reasoning skills and Mercury indicates intelligence. Therefore, such individuals are very strong in these skills and they take appropriate decisions based on the circumstances. Mercury is fond of learning and this conjunction indicates that the native is always ready to learn. Their brain works fast to understand the technology and other complex matters. Such conjunction provides strong communication skills with a strong ability to judge the situation and do negotiations accordingly.

If such conjunction is influenced by malefic then they become extremists. They use their intelligence for their gains and can go up to any extent. Their ideas are beyond the imagination of others, but when they cross the limits then the highly benefic planet starts giving their negative results. A strong Jupiter does not allow the person to go on the wrong path and the conscience of the person does not allow any negative work to be done. But if Jupiter is weak then negative results of such a combination are likely to be possible.

In fire signs, such a person is very benign and ready to help others. In Aries they are impulsive, in Leo they keep a distance from others and in Sagittarius, they like to study literature and prefer travel.

In earth signs, they are a very responsible and honest person. They are very stubborn in Taurus, flexible in Virgo, and have a changeable approach in Capricorn.

Air signs give birth to an extremely intelligent person. A powerful conjunction placed in air signs gives birth to an extraordinary mind, a person of noble character with strong business acumen.

Water signs indicate a person who can think deeply. The qualities of Jupiter are profound and Mercury also feels comfortable. Therefore, a person of a sharp mind with benevolent nature is seen here.

Jupiter wants a person to follow the path of spirituality, but Mercury does not like such a path. If such a person becomes crazy about money, Jupiter removes his protective shield. Without guidance, such a person is unable to take proper decisions and wastes all the resources.

8.5 Jupiter – Venus

Both planets are considered as highly benefic in astrology and both are masters. Jupiter is considered to be the guru of the gods and Venus is the guru of the demons. When two gurus meet, pure knowledge is born. It indicates meeting of masculine and feminine energy at one place. Hence, it is a good conjunction and such person creative abilities are very high. They can give birth of new and innovative thoughts, new wisdom, and new establishment. Such people able to keep balance in life as these two energies cooperate with each other to achieve higher spiritual goals of life but if the matter is related with material world then they also fight with each other as husband and wife support each other but also fight with each other.

It is written in our texts that Jupiter treat Venus as its enemy but Venus's behaviour towards Jupiter is neutral. Venus is exalted in the twelfth house which is the house of Jupiter, so the question is why Jupiter considers Venus as its enemy?

The 12th house is the house of salvation where there is supreme knowledge and the lord of that knowledge is Brihaspati. But the path to attain that knowledge is provided by Venus. Therefore, Jupiter hates the lower activities of Venus. A person who wastes his sexual energy is far away from the path of spirituality and consequently far away from Jupiter. When a person indulges in lust and luxury, such a combination does not give its fruitful results and Jupiter starts considering Venus as its enemy and chaos is witnessed in the life of the native related to the concerned house.

But when a person lives a spiritual life and utilize such energy on higher aspects then Venusian energy support the person to gain knowledge and wisdom. When such energy moves in upward direction then it will reach its exaltation house. Such a person is proficient and knowledgeable in many arts and subjects. They are very kind by nature. Knowledge is always their first priority and money come later. Both the planets help in improving the economic condition of the native, as they are proficient in many arts, hence they have different sources of income.

Fire signs indicates high energy which should always be used in a constructive way. Earth signs indicate that they are wealthy, loyal and dutiful individuals. They always do their work with full responsibility and do not take any decision in haste.

The air signs are friendly, wind expands rapidly, so their imaginations are very high. But such energy gives its negative consequences if not controlled properly.

Jupiter feels comfortable in water sign. They think creatively and have the ability to do something new.

8.6 Jupiter – Saturn

It is also known as the Great Conjunction as it happens once in about twenty years. Jupiter represents expansion and Saturn represents restrictions, diseases, and death. It is the meeting of two contradictory energies that indicates the beginning of a new cycle. The behavior of both planets is neutral to each other. They are polite and calm. Etiquettes and manners are their priorities. They are a very religious and courageous person.

The journey starts from the Sun and ends to Saturn. In between, there is an expansion of life. Every day Jupiter is protecting us and every day our life moves towards Saturn. One who knows such truth supports the two contradictory energies. Hence, the person having such conjunction becomes philosophical. They are very religious and benevolent. They have a balanced outlook and are always down to earth. They have their own principles and have strong beliefs about them. They are good at planning and delegate their work only when they find a trustworthy person, otherwise, they prefer to do it by themselves. They want to live with dignity but are never ready to do any wrong things.

They can easily understand rules and regulations and work in legal matters. They keep a record of everything and never forget anything easily. They are very punctual, strictly follow the rules and know the limitations, and do not allow anyone to cross the limits. They can't tolerate anything and give a good lesson who try to cross limits. Soon, people aware of their restricted behavior and they follow it in every matter of life.

But sometimes at home, their behavior creates a problem for others because they want that others will also follow their rules. They have leadership abilities and tend to dominate others.

Fire signs indicates disturbances in the life of a person. They want to change the rules and are not ready to follow the old system or conservatism prevailing in society. They love the new system and they work hard to change it. Jupiter- Saturn indicates the beginning of a new cycle in the fire sign.

Earth signs indicate limitations and Saturn means restrictions. Hence, Jupiter's energy gets limited here; Such a person becomes obedient and disciplinary in life. They are frugal because they understand the meaning of every rupee, but if Jupiter is badly placed then they become a miser.

The struggle between two opposite energies is high in the air signs. Due to Mercury's lordship and dual nature, Jupiter does not like Gemini. Libra is the marketplace that is also not liked by Jupiter. However, due to the humanitarian aspect, the element of Aquarius supports Jupiter. Saturn is a friend of Mercury, gets exalted in Libra, and is lord of Aquarius. So, the weightage shifts in favor of Saturn, and accordingly Saturnine influence is high in the air signs.

Water sign shows the religious tendency of a person. Water signs are also known as the sign of Moksha (Moksha) and both the planets bestow the person with great qualities. Such a person leads a very respectable and peaceful life and attains high knowledge.

8.7 Jupiter – Rahu

This yoga is known as Guru-Chandala Yoga and according to the scriptures it is not an auspicious yoga. Jupiter means; Spirituality, purity, honesty and such qualities are of no importance to Rahu and it takes interest only for his own benefit and for this he is ready to do anything. Rahu means outcast and rebellion. Rahu is not ready to follow the traditional way of living and thinking and is ready to break the rules.

Jupiter means honesty and Rahu is deceitful. Jupiter means that the person will work hard to clear the exam and Rahu means that the person will use mischievous activities. Jupiter is benevolent and always wants to give to others whereas Rahu is selfish and greedy and always wants to take from others.

These are two opposite forces. They do not like each other, but circumstances force them to live together in a house. Both the energies do not support each other. Therefore, the matter related to that house is always disturbed. Sometimes such a person associates with good and pious people of the society. Sometimes he falls from the right path in life and associates with bad or outcast persons. Rahu also gives temptation to cheat others. If such conjunction is very close and less than 8 degrees, then the person has company of bad friends and spend time in mischievous and unsocial activities. In such a situation, the qualities of Jupiter are reduced and the qualities of Rahu become strong.

In the present-day, Rahu represents the new and modern technologies which have broken many old and traditional systems and has changed the entire world. Rebellions (Rahu) are not ready to follow the traditional system and according to them all these are superstitions. Nowadays people are ready to break the rules indicates the influence of Rahu in the present world.

Because the person of this conjunction is always on the lookout for new ideas, he can catch the changing trends easily but due to the confusion of Rahu he is not able to take the right decision, he needs the help of Jupiter for proper direction. This conjunction also indicates the conversion of old scriptures into soft copies which we are reading in our laptops and a small chip can keep record of thousands of books.

Jupiter is noble and polite. Rahu represents anarchy and ready to break any boundary. When there is a change from an old system to a new system, chaos first arises. Rahu is forceful, so people want to break the old and outdated system. The person having such conjunction has the capacity to pave the path for a new system. But change is not easy and this conjunction indicates the tussle between two opposite energies.

Rahu is known to break the traditions and rules. Rahu doesn't listen anyone's advice and feels himself supreme. Rahu is also known to change his face quickly. When situated with Jupiter, Rahu occupied his qualities but only to show and cheat others. He knows that in the company of scholars he is an outsider. Hence, he wants to change the rules but want to convert it in his favour.

For example, if such a conjunction is formed in the 7th house, the person does not believe in marriage and may go for a live-in relationship or marriage against the traditions. But when he finds that such a relationship is of no use, he does not hesitate to break the relationship.

If such a combination is in the 11th house, then the person is related to mischievous people. He does not like the regular way of earning and works hard to develop a new technique which is highly supported by modern technology.

Such conjunction indicates that the person will suffer from a setback in life. Due to his rebellious nature, he will suffer and find it difficult to give respect to teachers and elders. Therefore, to reduce the negative effects of such a combination, one should develop the quality of reading good books and respect one's elders and masters.

Such a conjunction indicates that a person has the ability to do something new. The presence of Jupiter shows that conscience is alive. A book in the wrong hand does not mean the book has lost its value. How to use such knowledge is decided by the individual. God has given the choice of path in the hand of man, he can choose either Rahu or Jupiter. The choice of option decides the fate of the individual. Hence, Moon plays an important role, it is our mind that decide which path the person will choose.

8.8 Jupiter – Ketu

Ketu bestows powerful insight, concentration, deep penetration, and capacity for research and findings. When Ketu's energy meets with Jupiter, the planet of spirituality and knowledge, it gives birth to true seekers. Ketu is headless and karaka of Moksha. It indicates we can't go on the path of God with our head which means with our ego. A person has to surrender his ego only then can he seek the true path of spirituality. This conjunction is called "Ganesha Yoga".

Ketu bestows the person with intuition and clairvoyance. This conjunction indicates that the instinct of a person is high and takes interest in learning and research-related activities. For acquiring knowledge and doing research one has to sit in one place with total concentration and these persons have such qualities. As age grows, they become highly religious and like to read religious literature and practice meditation. Such conjunction also indicates an inclination towards occult sciences.

The headless planet doesn't bother about the activities in the outer world, hence they are not greedy for money. They want to go deep and they can find the hidden truth. The energy of Ketu works for separation. Hence, they do not feel attachment related to the matter of the concerned house and keep everything secret.

Such conjunction gives birth to a mysterious person whose actions are unknown to others. They work in secret and do not share their views with others. They have the strong power to assimilate any mystery. The functioning of Ketu is mysterious, indicating that one quietly indulges in his findings, knowledge, and research. They keep working towards their goal without informing anyone. Before moving on to the next level, they filter the communication and give only the information they find necessary.

Ketu represents all secret activities whether it is positive or negative. Therefore, if such energy is not turned into spiritual activities, then negative outcomes are possible from such conjunction. They can misuse their knowledge of secret sciences. They may secretly harm others and not reveal their true face. Everything they do is hidden and in the dark. The conjunction which has the quality of producing a great seeker of truth can also take a person to the abyss.

Rahu and Ketu both are disturbed energies and the placement of these nodes indicates that the matter related to that house is always disturbed. Hence, the person never sticks with one principle, Ketu's energy separates them and they move from one direction to another.

The position of Ketu indicates that the person has already experienced the matter related to the house and does not like to take any pressure there. If someone forces him then he is ready to leave it forever, because he lacks any attachment to the matters related to that house. On the path of truth, one has to give up all the feelings of the mundane world and this is the higher aspect of this conjunction.

Chapter 9

Transit of Jupiter

The transits of slow-moving planets have a long-term effect on the life of the native and among these the transit of Jupiter is very important as it is considered to be the most beneficial planet in astrology. Jupiter stays in one sign for a year and completes one revolution in 12 years. According to the Vimshottari Dasha system, human life is 120 years, which means that every human has only ten rounds of Jupiter (12*10=120 years). With the completion of each cycle of Jupiter, one moves toward the next level of maturity.

Therefore, 12, 24, 36, 48, and 60 years are very important in our life. Hence, after every 12 years there is maturity within us and after the completion of every rotation of Jupiter, many important changes take place. It also means that our time is running out and after 60 years half of our time is over.

Therefore, after 60 years people retire from their mundane activities. The planet of wisdom says that now you have to change your life cycle. Till now one's energy is focused on the material world but now the time has come to focus on the inner world. Jupiter is the lord of Pisces where there is supreme knowledge and without the blessings of Lord Jupiter no one can take even a step towards it. Jupiter is an asset and our every action that pleases Him is also an asset. Therefore, we should always do such work so that the blessings of Jupiter are always with us.

The transit of Jupiter affects the physical and spiritual life of the native. It depends on what you are looking for in life and how hard you have worked towards your goal. One cannot attain supreme knowledge if he has not sought it. When Jupiter transits over the natal planets and forms an aspect with other planets, then multiple events take shape in the life of the person.

The position of Jupiter in a house provides expansion and its aspect provides support. Out of the three aspects, its 7th aspect is considered to be highly beneficial. When a person is waiting for the good days of his life, then the 7th aspect of Jupiter on his Moon sign is the beginning of the golden days.

Jupiter's Transit on Different Houses

9.1 First House

The transit of Jupiter in the first house brings happiness in the life of a person. The solution of many pending problems starts coming and the life of the person starts getting easier. From here Jupiter views the seventh house. Hence the native may get married or the relationship with the partner becomes healthy. The person may develop a tendency to eat more sugar and have diabetes. This can also happen when Jupiter transits over ascendant lord. The first house represents head and brain and Jupiter protects the person from any head-related injury. It is the house of name, fame and prestige and with the blessings of Jupiter one is able to attain it.

9.2 Second House

The transit of Jupiter in the second house helps a person to increase income and savings. This is the house of jewellery, precious stones, and other exchangeable asset, Jupiter bestow the person to achieve such things in life. This brings happiness in the family and during this period family disputes get resolved. The native can buy valuables and becomes able to increase his social status. From here the Jupiter's aspect is on the eighth house, which is the house of debt, so the person gets the loan easily. But he can take too much loan and later he may face problem in repaying it. The native make harmony with everyone at home. Success comes easy and it makes a person arrogant.

9.3 Third House

It is the house of communication and writing. The transit of Jupiter indicates that the native will see an increase in such qualities in life. It is the house of courage and short travel. The native will take initiative in those areas of life, which he thought many times till now that he should take such a step. Jupiter provides the direction to choose the right path and short-term travel is enhanced. Correspondence and documents related activities increase and the native builds good relations with his neighbours. From here the aspect of Jupiter is on the ninth house which is the house of religion, higher education and long journeys. Therefore, activities in these matters of life also increase. This is the house of the subconscious mind where people plant their desires; hence the transit of Jupiter influences our hidden interests and inclinations.

9.4 Fourth House

It is the house of comfort, dreams and happiness and the transit of Jupiter indicates an increase in such activities. The native is able to fulfill his long-held dreams. The relations between the family members are cordial and they support each other. This house represents chest; hence, health-related problem also gets improved. This is the house of the masses and the person gets respect from the public. This is the house of immovable property and during this time the person can buy a new vehicle.

This is the nadir point of the zodiac and one takes interest in meditation and learning esoteric science. From here Jupiter looks upon the tenth house, so the environment of the work place is also helpful to the person. It is the house of all our roots, so one takes interest in family values and is connected to the homeland. The native takes interest in doing all those activities which give him mental peace and emotional satisfaction.

9.5 Fifth House

It is the house of creativity; hence, the expansion of creativity is seen at different levels and the aspect of Jupiter on the fifth lord also gives fruitful results. Jupiter bestows the person with children because they are our creation. From here, Jupiter makes trine relation with the 9th house and ascendant. Hence, it is the highest benefic placement and motivates the person towards literary activities. It is the house of counseling and a strong fifth house is essential to be a good advisor. Fifth house is for entertainment, speculation, gambling and change in job. The transit of Jupiter indicates that the time has come to fulfill such a desire but expansion should be controlled otherwise unnecessary bets may cause harm. The native will see an increase in income and good support from his network as Jupiter is aspecting the 11th house here.

9.6 Sixth House

The transit of Jupiter through the sixth house gives success in competition. The person is able to complete various pending tasks of his daily life. There are less conflicts and obstacles in life and the person resolves his disputes and gets success in legal matters. The person may develop some peculiar taste and change in food habits are possible.

A strong house indicates a good immune system, so the problem related to immunity will improve and the person will see good progress towards his health. This house is related to eating habits and one will like to eat more fatty and sweet products and diseases may develop as Jupiter gives expansion. The person will get respect from his subordinates and servants. The native may travel to religious places and expenses may also increase.

9.7 Seventh House

The transit of Jupiter in the seventh house brings many auspicious results. The native gets married and enters into a new relationship. The 7th house to the 12th house represents the outside world and the transit of Jupiter indicates an increase in the activities of the outside world.

This house indicates how a person presents himself to the outside world and Jupiter means a humble and knowledgeable person. The person is able to speak in public and take care of his image. It is the house of war, rewards, trade contracts and agreements and a positive development can be seen from all these fronts. It is the house of all kinds of relations, whether legal or illegal and Jupiter indicates that such relations are pious and for a noble purpose. Such a person is ready to cooperate and negotiate for mutual benefit.

9.8 Eighth House

It is house to the unexpected things in life. Serious and unknown diseases, difficulties and changes are visible from here. The planets placed here play an important role in a person's life and indicate that the life of a person will not be stable and there will be many ups and downs. If the planets are placed in this house then the transit of Jupiter plays an important role as various hidden activities start on the positive front in the life of the person whose results come suddenly.

This house represents the in-laws and the person gets support from there. It is the house of inheritance and unexpected wealth, which one can get with the blessings of Jupiter. It is the house of research and investigation, occult and hidden science and spy related activities. The person involved in such activities may get the results of his search. It is the house of retirement, insurance, pension and gratuity and one can see an increase in activities on these fronts.

At such a time, one may get money held back for a long time. From here Jupiter looks upon the second house which is the house of savings and the person will be able to increase it. The transit of Jupiter in the eighth house protects a person from any untoward incident in life.

9.9 Ninth House

It is the house of religion, faith and knowledge. With the transit of Jupiter, the native's inclination towards religion increases and he takes interest in literary works. It is the house of luck and Jupiter brings luck. This is the house of the father and the person gets the support of his father and superiors. This is a very favorable transit and the person undertakes a long journey for higher education.

The planets placed in the ninth house make a person intelligent and the transit of Jupiter helps in expanding their knowledge. The native will travel to holy places and take interest in philosophy. It is the house of invention, discovery and exploration and one will see an increase in activities on these fronts in life. Since it is the home of foreign affairs, activities related to these fronts also see an expansion. This house creates fanaticism and the transit of Jupiter increases the fanatical tendency of a person.

9.10 Tenth House

It is known as midheaven, the highest point of the zodiac. The Sun touches the mid-sky point every day at noon, so the activities related to the house are highly visible. It is the house of karma and is also known as the Upachaya house which means that the planets located here contribute to the growth of an individual. Among the body parts, the tenth house represents the knees which provides movement. When the planet of expansion enters this house, the work starts speeding up. The person gets promotion and success in his endeavors. He is a respected person in the organization and people listen to him. The activities at the workplace become hectic and the person gets appreciation from their work.

It is the house of rules and commandments and Jupiter makes new rules which is beneficial for others. Work and discrepancies related to this house are highly visible and if a person indulges in wrong deeds, then Jupiter removes his protective shield, then the person has to face various problems related to work. It is the house of profession, source of livelihood, ambition, public image, glory etc. Hence, a strong 10th house is essential for a successful career in life. Jupiter's transit to this house is a very auspicious time and one should use such time in a constructive manner as it is available only for a year.

9.11 Eleventh House

It is the house of income, profit and fulfillment of desires and the entry of Jupiter indicates increase in one's income and fulfillment of desires. The native makes new friends and improves his public image. He can become a good spokesperson and can give good presentation in an assembly or meeting. Jupiter helps the person to get back the lost money.

It is the house of attachment, affection and excessive indulgence for material gains. Inauspicious planets placed in this house indicate excessive indulging in anti-social activities and material pursuits of the native, such activities may increase and the desires of the person may be out of control.

If Rahu is present then chaos will develop in the person's life as these are two opposite energies. It is the house to the playground and one takes interest in outdoor sports. It is the house of networking, electronic media, modern technology, collaboration and social activities and one can see an increase in activities on all these fronts.

9.12 Twelfth House

It is the home of spiritual liberation, solitude and meditation. The transit of Jupiter enhances the activities related to this house. The native starts taking interest in meditation and spiritual practices. It is the house of expenditure and the person suddenly sees an increase in expenses. This house indicates the secret working of the mind and Jupiter protects the person from any conspiracy, manipulation and fraud. This house represents foreign land and if there is any possibility of going abroad now is the time. It is the house of misfortune and Jupiter protects the person from any misfortune in life.

The afflicted 12th house can put the person in hospital or jail. Jupiter protects a person from imprisonment, exile and accidents. If a person follows a noble path in life, then Jupiter's protective shield is available to him. The twelfth house indicates loan repayment and with the blessings of Jupiter the person is able to repay his debts.

Note: Not only the transit of the planet matters but also the conjunction and aspect with the planets in the natal chart also matters. To trigger an event all the nine planets combined energy works. Hence, sometimes the transit is unable to deliver the expected results. If the conjunction or aspect is not powerful or any negative energy works then the outcome of the transit will change. Also, it is necessary to check the points obtained in the Ashtakvarga System.

Chapter 10

Nakshatras of Jupiter

Vedic astrology considers the influence of 27 nakshatras on the earth which is divided into 12 equal parts, thus span of each nakshatra is 13 degrees 20 minutes. This span is further divided into 4 parts, each part is called pada which spans 3 degrees 20 minutes. Moon moves 13.2 degrees in a day i.e., it complete the full cycle of zodiac in 27.3 days (360°/13.2°). Every planet is lord of three nakshatras and Jupiter is lord of Punarvasu, Vishakha and Purva Bhadrapada.

The energy for all the three Jupiter nakshatra is works for creation, so what is the difference between these energies?

- Punarvasu indicates creation through repetition.

- Vishakha indicates creation through transformation.

- Purva Bhadrapada indicates creation through destruction.

10.1 Punarvasu

Punarvasu is the 7th nakshatra and is situated at 20° 00' Gemini - 3° 20' Cancer. The word Punarvasu comes from the two words 'Punar' and 'Vasu'. Punar means 'Again', 'Afresh', 'Another', or 'Anew' and Vasu means 'Bright', 'Excellent', 'A ray of light', 'Beneficial', or 'Wealth'. Hence, Punarvasu means 'Bright again', 'Wealthy again', 'Another ray of light', 'Afresh again' or 'Excellent again'.

Characteristics: Punarvasu people are generous and magnanimous people and are always ready to help others. They are soft-spoken, social, friendly, and humorous people. They provide support to everyone whom they see in difficulty. They readily give their goods to others who need them. They know the right use of available resources and can create something new with limited resources and never complain about the lack of resources. They are protectors and do their duties very well.

They are benign and like to do charity. If someone demands something from the Punarvasu people then he never returns empty-handed. They are simple, benevolent, and maintain good relations with everyone. They are intelligent and never harm others.

Punarvasu people are kind and humble, their life makes them humble. The ego is like a rock, where everything is fixed, but rocks become sand through weathering and erosion over the years. Success is difficult for Punarvasu people in the first attempt and this gives birth to a very determined and humble person who learns from the roller-coaster ride of life.

Since this energy supports many attempts, therefore, one thing is certain and that is success in the first attempt is doubtful. But Punarvasu is not for taking only one attempt. They do not take interest in those works in which only one attempt or limited attempt is available. Because their talent does not come out properly, they don't show any interest in doing such work or quit very soon.

They don't like any monotonous work that doesn't offer any challenge to their mind. They say, "Try this and try that...", they like to sit late at night on the table to solve the problem. Till the problem exist their mind can't take peace and they continuously think about various possibilities to resolve it. The symbol of the constellation signifies that the "Quiver is full of arrows"; So, they don't want any kind of restrictions. It is better to give them a free hand and such people will give their best results if you try to limit them then they will leave it.

They prefer to go for jobs like computer programming, scientific research, music, sports, etc., where many attempts are required before the final result. This type of work allows them to make proper use of their talent. They love to hone their skills; 'Practice makes a man perfect' is his motto. More effort means a sharp mind and a shining personality, then they show their success with gusto.

They believe that failure means coming close to success. Like a mother encouraging her child to get up when he falls, they always inspire others to keep trying.

After multiple failures, frustration is obvious to anyone but not to Punarvasu people. They never get discouraged and come back again with full energy. They will keep doing it until they get success. They become passionate to get the desired thing and forget day and night, forget food and clothes, forget friends and relations. They constantly throw their arrows to hit the target.

It may be possible that such a person may lose everything in that process but they never lose their hope and they can get it back. By the grace of Jupiter, a new ray of light comes into their life and they are re-established with renewed vigour.

Punarvasu persons are those who always motivate their team members to make another attempt. They often say, "I know that you can do it, try one more time and do your best". They respect talents and provide proper support. They never shout about failures and when they find that people are disheartened then they make the situation pleasant by using their jovial behaviour.

The ancient sages have given the Vaishya (Merchant) caste to this nakshatra. A merchant should be firm on his decisions and ready to explore unknown territory. When nothing is visible to others, he can see what is hidden and what is coming, and once he decided to go ahead, he should not deviate his mind from external forces. Because every decision cost money and for a merchant every rupee is important. One who does not know the value of money can't become a good merchant. Punarvasu people have all these qualities.

Punarvasu native always looks fresh and their mind is always ready for the next attempt. Their subconscious mind is always traveling to explore; Hence, they are always ready for a trip and surprise others by making untimely visits.

It is very difficult for Punarvasu people to sit idle in one place. They like to roam here and there, discuss with everyone and make the environment pleasant with their humorous behaviour. They are very social, have many friends, and mingle easily with others. Such a person likes to wander around and prefers a job where short travelling is involved. In their discussions, they often use the term; Trip, Tour, Transit, Ride, Run, and Go. They have a lot of energy to travel and if Mars is situated in this Nakshatra, then such a person can walk miles on his feet.

They are very good at time management and after completing one task, they immediately move to another task and have the ability to complete the third one in between. They reach just before the commencement of the process or journey and never miss the bus.

This Nakshatra has the potential to make one an expert as it is not only making many attempts but also knowing the various causes of failures. By the time the person reaches the result, he has experienced many things in life. Such a person can become a great master in his life.

On the higher aspect, searching into the territory of the unknown is not easy. Where no one knows anything about the way, direction, and necessary resources. Then a person decides to find solutions that seem ridiculous to others. But the thought of seeking is so intense for these people that if he does not work in that direction, he cannot sleep peacefully and then the search begins.

This energy signifies that after so many lives wandering in this material world, one starts searching for the 'unknown' which is present everywhere but not visible to the eyes. The person starts searching around and asks everyone who has seen "Him". When the thirst for the "unknown" begins, this energy compels the individual to seek and cannot stop until he finds the "Ultimate Truth".

Lord Ram was born in this nakshatra. Their story tells us how strong this nakshatra is in doing 'good again' in the life of the person.

Negative Traits: Punarvasu people have the strength to solve complications and this pleasures their minds. Therefore, they often like to invite complexity and feel happy to be involved in that matter. Sometimes they make a simple matter very complicated and run around to solve it.

Because deep down in their subconscious mind they want to run. Wandering unnecessarily is not good, so they deliberately create confusion and like to run away. In that process, they involve others and love to show off their problem-solving skills. They assign some tasks to everyone to reduce the problem and when everyone is busy, they feel satisfied.

They are always ready to go somewhere, whether their health or other situation allows it or not, they are not ready to listen to anyone. They blame others who do not support their plan. They are fickle-minded people and do not like anything stable in life, not even relationships. They do not like to stay in one place for a long time and like to change the place or city or country.

10.2 Vishakha

Vishakha is the 16th of 27 nakshatras and situated at 20° Libra – 3° 20' Scorpio. The Sanskrit word Vishakha has come from two words – the first is "Vi" which means "Divided" and "Shakha" which means "Branch". It means a branch that is forked or divided into two parts. It also means a two-way path is merged into a single path and indicates one point or one direction. It is known as "The Star of Purpose". It's another name is "Radha".

This is the only constellation in which one planet (Saturn) is exalted and the other (Moon) is debilitated. Fair division is needed to properly divide an object into two parts and only an impartial person can do that. Justice means balance, hence, the lord of justice – Saturn, find this place perfectly fit as per his disposition and exalted at 20°, at the onset of this nakshatra.

The last pada of this nakshatra comes under the sign of Scorpio, which is the darkest, most poisonous, and most dangerous part of the zodiac. Moon, the planet of emotions, feels extremely uncomfortable at this place and becomes debilitated at 3°.

Characteristics: Vishakha Nakshatra people are highly focused on their objective. They are very determined person and become ruthless to achieve their desires. They are goal-oriented people, play gimmicks, always tense, and want to finish the task within the limited time frame. Hence, they often use the word "target" and "deadline" in their discussion. They are always conscious about their image, so they always dress elegantly and believe that success requires an impressive outfit.

They are passionate, clever, daring, and fearless people, and are known for their courage. They are intelligent, attractive, and good-looking people and females of Vishakha look very beautiful and charming. They are hard-working people and love adventure. They are very confident people and sometimes they take wrong decisions due to overconfidence. They are always suspicious on others and find it hard to trust anyone.

They have little regard for the rules and regulations that restrain their free-spirited nature. They are impulsive, lively, dynamic and want to be the center of attention at social gatherings. One moment they look furious and the next they become calm and emotional. It is very difficult to predict their movement and a person never knows what their next move is going to be.

The exaltation of one planet and the debilitation of another planet in this sign indicates that in one aspect of life they reach the pinnacle and in the other aspect their life touches the abyss. There is another meaning of this exaltation and debilitation; There is a time their life touches the bottom and no one is paid any attention them; Then when time changes and their life touches the pinnacle, everyone likes them.

They show complete integrity in doing their work and like to do things efficiently and accurately. They have a strong throat and can speak for hours. They have the quality to become good orators and speakers. They are great motivators and have a strong capacity to bring passion and enthusiasm among team members.

Due to their strong vocal power, they dislike small discussions and want to speak more in a meeting. They do not like to listen to others and for them others are there only to listen to them. They are highly professional and maintain a high standard in business dealings. They have a bossy attitude and always want to give order. They keep an eye on every development and never miss any minuscule detail. They are best in those jobs where sharp instincts are required, such as lawyers, investigators, spokespersons, etc.

Vishakha means a branch that is divided into two, hence, they believe in diversification and at a time they indulge in many projects. But underneath of all they have single-mindedness and use the power of aggression to achieve their target. They are highly dedicated to their aim and wait patiently to achieve the outcome. To fulfill their desire, they can wait for years without intimating anyone.

The Mleccha (Outcaste) caste of this nakshatra indicates, on the lower aspect, they take interest in underworld activities and those acts which are not generally done by the common people.

On a higher aspect, they take interest in occult science and like to do various occult practices in remote places. It represents a bandit and a hermit, both are opposite to each other, but both are not able to live in society. A bandit is one whose energy is high but the direction is wrong and a hermit is one whose energy is high in the right direction and exactly the lordship of Jupiter of this nakshatra represents this. They have the potential to go high if they chose the right direction in life.

As per Hindu mythology, the character of Valmiki perfectly fits with this nakshatra. The two branches of Vishakha indicate that one has to see the dark phase of life before one can see the light or become a hermit. When a person can control the negative energy then it transforms and moves in the upward direction and that direction is provided by Jupiter (Guru), as after getting the direction from sage Narada a robber Ratnakar turned into sage Valmiki.

Negative Traits: They are very talkative people, like to gossip and pry into other people's things. They don't like boundaries and restrictions and are ready to cross them to fulfill their desire. They often lose their close friends due to their adamant behaviour. They are always in a hurry and show that they are very busy.

They often say "fast-fast" with their colleagues and co-workers in the organization. They don't trust anyone and prefer to work alone. They don't like to take advice from others, they are stingy and ready to take revenge. They are greedy and ready to manipulate things for their benefit.

They are fond of material pleasure. They are sex obsessed and want to enjoy finer things in life. They make promises but never bother about its fulfillment. They are always looking for profits and when the situation is not in their favour they easily take U-turns regardless of the loss of others and hesitate to fulfill their obligations.

They are party lovers and prone to drugs and alcohols. They are not blessed with love from family. They fail in relationships because they say one thing and do the exact opposite. Their marital life also gets disturbed and break-up is possible as they never give importance to their spouse as both Indra and Agni, the deities of this Nakshatra, wooed other wives.

10.3 Purva Bhadrapada

Purva Bhadrapada is the most intense of all the 27 nakshatras and is situated at 20° Aquarius – 3° 20' Pisces. Bhadra means - One who brings welfare and luck; Pada means feet and Purva means former or before. Hence, it means "One who brings luck before" or "The first lucky step".

The person who takes the first step on the path of spirituality is extremely fortunate and the name of the constellation indicates this. But before taking that "First lucky step" one must know the futility of the material world, and this requires an experience of burning. Until one burns his fingers, the worldly attraction keeps on pulling him. Only one experience of burning is enough to take that first step lucky step and such a person jump immediately into spirituality without having a second thought. Hence, this constellation has a strong connection with fire and burning. Purva Bhadrapada is known as lightning in the sky between thunderclouds.

Characteristics: The energy of Purva Bhadrapada is like a double-edged sword. It is like a storm that is ready to destroy anything but still remains wet and can prove to be a boon for areas facing summer drought. It is a very powerful transformative energy that can change the seasons. Planets in Purva Bhadrapada indicates changes are inevitable in the life of the person.

It is a highly destructive and ruthless energy which shows no mercy to anyone. Purva Bhadrapada people believe that creation can be done only after destruction. The new will come but before that old has to go and they are the initiators of removing anything which has become obsolete and dead. They break all their ties with one that has lost its relevance. They do not take any time to break those relationships which are of no use today and burn all the memories and pictures.

Many times, people get stuck in old rules and regulations, culture and traditions which have lost its value but people do not dare to take it out from their home, their society, their culture or from their country, then Purva Bhadrapada enters and revolution begins. People get furious and start shouting to throw out the old system. The process of creative destruction begins, fire and gusty wind (heated discussions) spreads everywhere. Purva Bhadrapada people do those courageous acts which others are afraid to do. It can happen into a family, into a society or into a country but Purva Bhadrapada is ultimately able to take the corpses (dead beliefs and rules) to the crematorium (out of the system).

When someone dies and the relatives are crying, but the dead body has to be taken to the crematorium. During this process, those who take the dead body to the cremation ground do not listen to anyone's cries and they are not kind to leave the body. The dead body has to be burnt, this is the act of purification and this has to be done.

Purva Bhadrapada people do not listen to anyone's advice or cries, they feel that what they are doing is always right. They think that it is necessary to do this and they are doing right job. Therefore, it is futile to cry in front of these people. They are merciless and ready to make sacrifices for what they think is a great cause. According to their opinion, sacrifice is necessary, they are doing something great act which will bring change to the system, and for that purpose they are ready to kill themselves and others. Hence, they often use the word "sacrifice is necessary", "sacrifice for change" and they believe that what they are doing is very pious and noble.

In general discussions they often say that they don't believe in outdated traditions and rules which has lost its relevancy. Even at home they don't like anything which is worthless or dead, they are ready to throw it immediately. They are ready to throw anything without asking others which has lost its relevancy. They look things in term of its usability and often use the word 'useful' or 'useless' in their conversion.

Purva Bhadrapada keeps no relationship with anything that is useless or expired, be it a person or an object. They are ready to give up their family traditions or even leave the family if the ideology of the family does not match with their principles. The people of Purva Bhadrapada have no attachment to anything that has become junk, whether it is an investment made by them or an old relationship. The energy of the constellation works for settlement or ending;

- This is the cut-off energy.

- Such a person has no attachment to the one who has expired, they immediately throw it.

- The thing that has lost its relevance, they don't want to pursue it.

- What has become useless, they start avoiding it, relationships too.

When a company is declared insolvent, the court issues an order that the insolvent company be wound up. The process of liquidation begins, which is a complicated process of selling off the company's assets and paying off its debts. This is the same process that is done to take the dead body to the crematorium on the funeral cot. Purva Bhadrapada people work in all these liquidation processes of the company. They work in various legal and financial departments and eventually bring the dead company to its destination.

They are the best in the process of dissolving something and many times they say that such matter should be dissolved quickly and why it is taking so much time. They never delay the matter voluntarily and also tell others to finish their work quickly. They are very hardworking people and hate procrastination. They follow up all their pending tasks properly. They always ask their team members about the latest follow-up. Because deep in their subconscious mind they know that time is running out and funeral cot is coming, hence, they prefer to take term insurance plan quickly. They can't wait for long to achieve their objective and quickly wants to see the outcome of their efforts.

Purva Bhadrapada people involved in the process of final settlement or ending of any process. In the stock market, they operate in the trade settlement cycle where shares move from the seller's account to the buyer's account and money moves from the buyer to the seller. They work for settlement of loan in financial department. They work as a perfectionist and have strong ability to catch anything wrong (mistakes). If anything written wrong in the document then Purva Bhadrapada people can't forward it and return the document back. They never compromise on anything dead in the system, hence, for that they are very rigid. It is a very powerful energy to move a dead thing out of nowhere.

Purva Bhadrapada people tend to throw away useless things immediately. They immediately throw away what has become garbage. It is like a vacuum cleaner that sweeps away dust with its powerful air. When the wind of Purva Bhadrapada starts the process of cleaning starts. In India, March and April are the month of Vasant (Spring) and Sun enters in this nakshatra on 4th March. At this time trees shed their old leaves and the wind carries them away. Whatever has become lifeless, nature itself cleans it.

The women of Purva Bhadrapada tend to clean everything in the house. They don't like anything that is of no use and occupying space, so they utilize the space perfectly. But their cleaning behavior sometimes becomes eccentric. They always check the expiry date of a product and when they find anything old or expired, they immediately throw it away.

In the corporate world, Purva Bhadrapada bosses immediately fire their non-performing employees. They don't want to keep anything that is useless. The place of a wasted item is the dustbin and no one like to keep the garbage on the table. Similarly, they fired their non-performing employees from the company and sometimes without giving any notice. They never think about their past loyalty and dedication. At present, the person is of no use and keeping him in the organization is like keeping garbage at the table.

When anything wrong happens or someone is doing anything wrong to make things dead, then the energy of the constellation immediately works to remove it. They are very honest and can't tolerate if someone is doing anything wrong, mixing something bad and outdated in the new one, etc. When something wrong is happening and comes to the notice of Purva Bhadrapada people, they immediately act to throw that wrong and they fight fiercely to remove it. Union leaders, revolutionaries are influenced by this Nakshatra who fight to remove anything wrong, dead or outdated.

When they see anything dead, they cannot tolerate it and the energy of the Nakshatra prompts them to remove that thing from the system. They can catch the mistakes easily, because they have strong vision to find the mistakes. If a document is getting damaged due to some mistake, then that mistake has to be rectified and they immediately catch the mistake or forgery in the document.

Counterfeit currency is a dead currency and it has to be removed from the system immediately. Therefore, they work at places that remove counterfeit currency from the system. As soon as this person touches the note, he immediately realizes that it is fake. This energy does not allow the dead to stay with the living, even if they are buried inside the wall for years. Anything dead cannot stay anywhere with the living, the dead must be burned and they will find it.

Purva Bhadrapada people have two faces and the one is totally different from the other. On the one hand; Mystery, occult, violence, cunningness, fierce anger and on the other hand; Honesty, benevolence, charity, penance, etc. Due to high energy, they are able to complete the most difficult tasks which other people are not able to do. They are very bold and don't care about the social taboos and do what they want to do.

The nakshatra energy works for both creation and destruction simultaneously. Hence, contradictory personalities witnessed in their character; Benevolence and ruthlessness, merciful and violent, sociable and secretive, helpful and rude, a very pleasant mannerisms and on the other hand they don't hesitate to cut the relations immediately, etc.

They are religiously inclined person and having philosophical tendencies. They believe in occult science and put energy to learn it. They take care of each and every member of the family. They protect their family and worry about the health of their acquaintances. They can do strong penance and take intense pain for worship without hesitation.

They are skillful in money making. They are great warriors, fight for the truth and can create a whirlwind. They are great writers who write on revolutionary topics. Due to strong throat, they chant religious hymns loudly, they are very skillful in speaking and can speak for hours. They are great orators who speak in a public about to change the system. They love listening to loud music and want to enjoy the thrill of life. They have the capacity to endure intense pain and find pleasure in torturing themselves. Once they decide to give up their food or medicine, then no one can compel them to take it.

Negative Traits: The energy of the nakshatra lacks any kind of mercy, hence, they become extremally violent and ruthless. They are fickle minded person and lack the power of foresight. They become gloomy and depressed quickly. They become very anxious, lose their temper and start shouting. They can be very harsh towards others and not ready to listen to anyone. They can adopt cynical attitude, can become eccentric then it is very difficult to control them. They are selfish people and maintain relations only till their purpose is fulfilled, after that they never recognize you.

Demons, tyrants, mass murderers, homicides, genocides, dangerous criminals, serial killers are associated with this nakshatra. They are ruthless and ready to die, but before that they can cause great destruction. The strange thing is that they consider all their actions are right and do not feel guilty for committing heinous crimes, and think all these acts are for purification. While doing those crimes, they feel something great inside, like Angulimala felt that he was doing a great job by killing people.

They show only one face at a time to others and keep the other face in dark. Being secretive in nature they keep their activities hidden from others. Their activities do not match to the traditional society and they involve in those work which generally do not follow by others. During the day they do their normal job but at night they can work for violent and criminal activities. They can practice black magic or engage in activities of destruction.

The people of Purva Bhadrapada have the ability to make big changes but can also do big harm. The energy of a Nakshatra has a destructive effect, therefore, when the action is started it must be sure that the consequences are not normal and the end result is beyond expectations, because no one can gauge the destructive power of Rudra.

One of the driving forces of a hurricane is heat energy and it dies down when it loses its energy source which is usually warm water. To prevent the destruction of Purva Bhadrapada natives it is good not to make them angry and remove all items near to them which can produce heat.

Chapter 11

Jupiter, Money and Life

There are two types of things in this world – Living and Non-living. Living things has sentiments and emotions, non-living things are dead and only follow the law of nature. Such as; humans and animals have emotions but metal, paper, money, fire, etc. have no emotions.

When I was writing this book then people asked me what is the meaning of honesty in present days. Those who are honest are suffer, dishonest and fraudsters are shines.

Yes, it is true that a person can get immediate gain of non-living thing if he adopts a wrong path in life. But human life is not the accumulation of non-living things at home. There is some great purpose behind that and every person has a responsibility to search for that purpose.

But many people think that there is no difference between living and non-living things. In fact, they give high priority to non-living things and do not give any value to others lives even their life too. They are ready to do anything to collect non-living things and ready to sell their soul in the market. An inanimate thing has value only as long as it is in our hands and another person becomes its owner as soon as it changes hands. A person spends his life in collecting these lifeless things and forgets the real purpose of life.

For example, when a robber robbed a bank and collected money, then the gun in his hand can't deny that it will not follow the order because the robber is a bad person and its bullet will not enter in the body of a saint because he is a good man. If the robber wants to purchase a car or a bungalow, then the money can't deny that it will not follow his order, money has no feelings. Fire in our home has no friendship with us, it can burn us too, no matter for how many years it is with us.

But humans and animals have feelings. A faithful dog can't bite you on the orders of a bad man, it only obeys the orders of its master. In material world, people can see the rise of a person with the help of non-living things and consider that the collection of non-living things as a measure of success. But this human life is not to collect the non-living things but to increase the awareness of the soul.

Money in the material world is like wheels of a car, without which you can't move, your vehicle of life will stand at one place. But collection of wheels is not the only aim of life. You have to pay attention to other parts of the car and put a lot of effort into making it. If your focus is only on collecting wheels, then after some time that person smacks of arrogance. Many people change their behavior once they have money, as their focus is only on collecting wheels.

But such a person doesn't have engine, steering, seat, car body etc. to protect, neither they put any focus on it in their life. Because these are worthless and a person who has short vision can say that the car moves only by the wheels. They don't have the vision to see the above, they only see the fast movement below. Look up at the sky, where millions of stars are moving without any struggle. They indicate that human beings have to do something else in their lives than collection of inanimate objects.

After some time, a person whose focus is only on collecting wheels has many wheels but he does not have the energy to do other things. Then only those people will come in contact who want a wheel in their life, others leave them forever. A young boy turns into an extremely egotistical boss and the value of the person is only till he is staying on the chair. That's why many people die soon after leaving the chair.

When the chair is gone, the respect is also gone and the energy to collect the wheels is also gone. Such a person completely taken aback by such a change in life. They want to seek a new direction, but they have no assets of Jupiter, it has too late in their life. This is a shock that their lives are not prepared to handle. This is a shock that their lives are not prepared to handle. The human mind cannot exist without a purpose, and now they have no purpose for living.

Remember, without direction there is no meaning of wheels. Such a person is totally missed the purpose of his life. He has no assets of Jupiter and remember Jupiter is protection. In the solar system, Mars is on one side of Jupiter and Saturn is on the other. This shows that when Jupiter's protective shield is removed, they immediately catch hold of you.

Chapter 12

Ways to Improve Jupiter

The activities go on auspiciously in our lives with the blessings of Lord Jupiter. It is very important to have auspicious Jupiter for success in life. Without Jupiter one always finds himself in dilemma and unable to take any decision, whatever decision such a person will take will always be in doubt. An astrologer can analyse the horoscope to know whether a person's Jupiter is auspicious or not but not every person can become an astrologer.

Many persons have question that how do they know that their Jupiter is auspicious or not and what to do when Jupiter is not auspicious. The following points throw some light to know whether a person's Jupiter is auspicious or not and what to do if it is not auspicious;

12. 1 What to do when Jupiter is not Auspicious

1. One should always respect his Guru.

2. Jupiter represents honesty. If you are honest then Jupiter is beneficial for you.

3. Jupiter provides direction. Therefore, one should never voluntarily mislead anyone, otherwise, Jupiter of such a person will become malefic. Providing proper guidance to others strengthens our Jupiter.

4. A positive Jupiter indicates that the person sets the right direction very soon and never steps in any wrong direction.

5. Be truthful to your profession. If you are lying and deceiving others then your Jupiter is not good. A person who does not fulfill his promise even after saying it again and again, indicates a weak and inauspicious Jupiter.

6. Jupiter is your wealth. That's why one should never embezzle someone's money. Always remember your promise to return the money of others.

7. A positive Jupiter indicates benevolent nature of the person. Such a person is always ready to help others. On the other hand, if you help others then your Jupiter will become auspicious.

8. A positive Jupiter indicates that such a person is religious. He reads and memorizes scriptures, texts and chant mantras easily.

9. A positive Jupiter indicates that the person tends to save lives. Such a person can never harm others and if a person saves life of others, then his Jupiter will become auspicious.

10. A malefic Jupiter indicates a person who shows his pride over little knowledge. Jupiter's nature is benevolence, so a knowledgeable person never shows his arrogance, he is always humble and ready to share his knowledge to the competent person.

11. A strong Jupiter indicates natural thrust of learning, while an inauspicious Jupiter indicates stereotyped behaviour. A malefic Jupiter indicates, such a person does not listen to anyone and without any knowledge, he feels himself supreme in every sphere of life.

12. No harm should ever be done to a pregnant woman because the fetus growing in the mother's womb represents the expansion of life.

When a person does negative acts then his Jupiter becomes malefic and the most auspicious and benevolent planet starts providing its negative results. We should always do every act to make our Jupiter strong.

Jupiter is the real wealth that every person should work hard to get. A strong Jupiter in a horoscope shows that such a person had done great deeds in his previous births.

On the highest aspect, Jupiter bestows the person with divine knowledge, a higher level of consciousness, reverence, and spirituality. Without a strong Jupiter, the path of wisdom and spirituality will always be closed for a person and his wandering in this mundane world will continue.

12.2 Never Blame Your Luck

I have seen that many people always say – "How unlucky I am". They always blame their luck and compare how lucky others are. When anything happens that they don't like, they start blaming their luck. They are ready to blame their luck on anything they don't like. I've noticed that "Bad Luck" or "How unlucky I am" is a very common word on every other person's tongue.

They feel satisfied after blaming their luck that they found a reason for such incidents in life. Such people get frustrated easily, they are unable to fight adverse circumstances and start crying easily. When anything happens that they don't like, they are ready to say quickly "It is my bad luck."

You must remember that your luck is your Jupiter. When you blame your luck, you are blaming your Jupiter. Such words prohibit you to think constructively. Blaming your luck starts the vicious cycle of your misfortune.

I remember an incident, I was working in an organization, and one day they asked me to leave the job. My boss said that, "Ajay, it is very bad luck that such things happened to you". I replied, "Don't worry, my luck always favors me". I quit that job, and it is only because of the grace of Lord Jupiter that I have been able to complete this book today. The following are some of my observations to those who always blame their luck;

- When you blame your luck, you are also blaming your Jupiter which is the lord of wisdom, wealth and direction, etc.

- When you blame your luck, wisdom will disappear from your life. I have seen that such people buy books but do not read them.

- When you blame your luck, wealth will disappear. I have seen that one who always blames his luck suddenly loses his gold ornaments.

- Jupiter provides direction and such a person lacks direction in life when he blames his luck. They keep wandering here and there. They go in one direction and after some time they change their direction. They start one business and when it is not performing, they start blaming their luck. Without Jupiter, the person will waste his time, energy, and money.

So, you should never blame your luck. It is your Jupiter that provides you direction, wealth and wisdom, etc. Without the grace of Jupiter, a person cannot understand the right direction in his life. Jupiter provides expansion and blaming one's luck will destroy the quality of expansion. Soon, such a person becomes narrow-minded and always confused in any matter of life. Such a person lacks the necessary skills to take important decisions in life.

12.3 Weak Jupiter and Remedies

Weak Jupiter indicates; excess fat in the body, lever-related problems, no interest in reading books, problem in education, no interest in religious activities, the problem with teachers, loss of gold, wrong charges of theft, diabetes, childless couple, etc.

Remedies for Jupiter:

- Read Vishnu Sahasranama Sthotram

- Eat turmeric

- Wear gold

- Spread knowledge and help students

- Read good books

- Take blessings for Guru and always respect

- Wear Yellow Sapphire or Pukhraj

- Be generous and help others

- Always guide others in the right direction and never mislead anyone

- Vedic Mantra - "Om Brim Brihaspataye Namah"

- Beej Mantra - "Om Gram Grim Grom Sah Gurve Namah"

Bibliography

Brihat Parashara Hora Sastra by Maharshi Parasara

Brihat Jatak, Translation by Prof. P.S. Sastri, Rajan Publications, New Delhi

Jatak Parijat, Translation by V. Subramanya Sastri, Rajan Publications, New Delhi

Bhavartha Ratnakar, Translation by B.V. Raman, UBS Publishers, New Delhi,

ABC of Indian Astrology, Prof. (Dr.) Nimai Banerjee, Published by Mrs. Kanti Banerjee, Cuttak

Fundamental Principals of Astrology, by Prof. K.S. Krishnamurti

Hindu Science of the Future by Harihar Majumder

Scientific Hindu Astrology Vol 1 &2 by P.S. Sastri

Brihaspati<https://en.wikipedia.org/wiki/Brihaspati> Accessed on 18th Sept 2022

Jupiter< https://www.space.com/> Accessed on 18th Sept 2022

Jupiter<https://www.universetoday.com> Accessed on 19th Sept 2022

What Is Jupiter? < https://www.nasa.gov/> Accessed on 19th Sept 2022

Jupiter reach opposition<https://earthsky.org/astronomy-essentials/jupiter-at-opposition-closest-brightest-best/> Accessed on 11th Dec 2022

About The Author

Ajay Srivastava is the founder of www.lotuswisdom.in and holds 'Bachelor of Science' from Deen Dayal Upadhyay Gorakhpur University, Gorakhpur (UP) and 'Masters Programme in International Business' from PSG Institute of Management, Coimbatore (Tamil Nadu).

He has extensive experience in the capital market as a Lead Analyst, Investment Banker, Consultant, and Advisor in identifying investment opportunities and formulating strategies. In his career, he has written various research notes and has done in-depth research from a commercial and financing point of view in multiple deals. With diverse industry experience and wide understanding, he started imparting his knowledge in the industry since 2013.

He has deep knowledge of graphology and since childhood he is very much interested in analyzing a person by handwriting and has analyzed the handwriting of hundreds of persons in his life. He is very much passionate to learn about astrology and palmistry in deep and has completed 'JyotirVid' and 'JyotirVisharad' in Astrology from Bharatiya Vidya Bhavan, Mumbai. His various research articles have been published in the renowned magazine "The Astrological eMagazine" and "Planets & Forecast.

Email ID: ajay.srivastava@lotuswisdom.in

Web Site: http://www.lotuswisdom.in/

Books Written by the Author

1. Psychology and Investment

2. Vedic Astrology: The Light of Wisdom

3. Midlife Crisis: An Astrological Appraoch

4. Jupiter: The Planet of Fortune

5. The Joy of Creation and Success

6. The Light of Nakshatras

7. Sun: The Supreme Creator

8. Astrology & Predictions

9. Animal Symbols of Nakshatras

10. Astrology & Profession

11. Rahu & Ketu: The Invisible & Mysterious Planets

12. Planets & Human Life

Astrology Courses

1. Vedic Astrology for Beginners {Level – 1 (Basics)}

Module – 1: Basics of Astrology

Introduction; The Zodiac; Elements

Module – 2: Signs

Meaning of the Signs, Elements of the Signs, Qualities of the Signs, Odd and Even Signs, Sheershodaya & Prishtodaya Signs, Direction, Colors, Caste, Fruitful and Barren Signs, Masculine & Feminine Signs, Places, Other Major Qualities

Module – 3: Houses

Meaning of the 12 Houses, Types and Classifications of Houses

Module – 4: Planets

Planets and their Characteristics, Planetary Relationship, Exaltation, Debilitation & Mooltrikona, Natural Karakas, Karakas in Jaimini Astrology

Module – 5: Planets in Groups

Natural Benefic and Malefic Planets, Gender; Color; Caste; Guna and Places; Planet and Tastes; Nature of Planet; Elements; Metals; Age; Cloth and Height; Vegetable and Fruits; Physical Constituents and Tendency; Maturity Age of Planets; Planetary Aspects; Seasons; Hora

Module – 6: Planetary Strengths and Weaknesses

Strength of Planets based on its degrees, Direction; Direction Strength; Maran Karaka Sthana; Yog Karaka; Vargottam Planet; Shadabala

Module – 7: Retrograde and Combust Planet, Gandanta

2. <u>**Vedic Astrology for Beginners {Level – 2 (Advanced)}**</u>

Module 1: Vimshottari Dasha System

Nakshatra and Planetary Lordship, Change of Dasa and Results

Module 2: Basics of Nakshatra

Deity, Animal Symbol, Caste, Activity, Gana, Guna, Gender

Module 3: Important Yogas

Know the 30 most important astrological combinations

Module 4: Ashtakvarga

Interpretation of Ashtakvarga Table

Module 5: Transit of Planets and their impact

Understand the effect of transit of Jupiter, Saturn, Rahu-Ketu

Module 6: Planets and Profession

Identify the influence of the planet and the direction of profession

Module 7: Weak Planets and Remedies

Identify the signal of weak planets and useful remedies

Module 8: Key Steps to Chart Interpretation

Course Offerings:

· 30 hours of live sessions (Level 1 & Level 2)

· Learn various astrological concepts with practical examples

· Mode – Online Classes; Recordings available

3. <u>Nakshatra Course</u>

Knowledge of Nakshatra is very important in astrology, without it one cannot understand how energy works and what will be the result of the transit of planets. Do not limit yourself to the movement of planets, explore the world of Nakshatra and understand the hidden secrets.

What You'll Learn

• How the knowledge of Nakshatra helps to understand the characteristics and negative traits of the person

• Effect of transit of planets and time of activation

• Meaning of each symbol and its influence

• Influence of the associated animal on the personality of the person

• When to start a new venture and when not to go ahead

• Related Profession

• Understand each concept with logic

Course Offerings:

• 60 hours of live sessions

• Learn various astrological concepts with practical examples

• Mode - Online Classes, Recordings available

• Medium - English

Contact Us:

Mobile No.: +91 9867837184

Blog: https://lotuswisdomonline.blogspot.com/

Email ID: ajay.srivastava@lotuswisdom.in

4. A Course on Animal Symbols of Nakshatras

In the ancient scriptures, a total of 14 animals are related to the 27 nakshatras, and the behavior of every person is limited to these 14 animals. To understand the various merits and demerits of a person, it is necessary to understand the different characteristics of these animals.

How to Utilize Such Knowledge

• You will be surprised to know that these animals decide whom we form a relationship in our life.

• These animals determine our relationships with our friends, our spouse, our partners, our juniors and superiors.

• This knowledge helps to channelize your energy in pursuit of higher goals in life.

• The human mind is a very complex creation and it is difficult to say why a person behaves in a certain way and why his behavior changes. Knowledge of animal traits can provide proper guidance in this regard.

Course Offerings:

• 30 hours of live sessions

• Learn various astrological concepts with practical examples

• Mode - Online Classes; Recordings available

Sun:
The
Supreme
Creator
A Research Work on
Astrological Aspects of the Sun
Ajay Srivastava

The Light
of
Nakshatras
A Comprehensive Work to Explain the
Functioning of 27 Mystical Energies
Ajay Srivastava

Jupiter:
The
Planet of
Fortune
Ajay Srivastava

Vedic Astrology
The Light of Wisdom
Astrology for Beginners,
Learn the Language of Stars
Ajay Srivastava

PSYCHOLOGY
AND
INVESTMENT
The Art of Investing in Stocks with an
Explanation of Human Psychology
AJAY SRIVASTAVA

The Joy
of
Creation and Success
Ajay Srivastava

Midlife
Crisis: An
Astrological
Approach
Understand The Timing Of Crisis,
Learn How To Turn A Crisis Into An Opportunity
Ajay Srivastava

Astrology
&
Predictions
Ajay Srivastava

Animal Symbols
of
Nakshatras
Ajay Srivastava

Planets
&
Human Life
Ajay Srivastava

Notes

9 789359 155791